GUIDE TO BUDDAHOOD

BEING A

STANDARD MANUAL OF CHINESE BUDDHISM

GUIDE TO BUDDHAHOOD

BEING A

STANDARD MANUAL OF CHINESE BUDDHISM

Translated by

REV. TIMOTHY RICHARD, LITT. D.

MEMBER OF THE ENGLISH BAPTIST MISSION;
SECRETARY OF THE CHRISTIAN LITERATURE SOCIETY;
CO-CHANCELLOR OF THE SHANSI IMPERIAL
UNIVERSITY WITH THE GOVERNOR OF THE PROVINCE

GYAN

Published by

Gyan Publishing House
5, Ansari Road
Daryaganj, New Delhi-110002
Phone: 011-47034999, 9811692060
E-mail: books@gyanbooks.com

Distribution Network
gyanbooks.com
India, USA, Canada, UK, Australia, France

ISBN : 978-81-212-2388-1 (PB)
First Published, 1907

2nd Impression 2021

Printed at: Gyan Press, Delhi.

Guide to Buddahood
Being A
Standard Manual of Chinese Buddhism
Translated by: Rev. Timothy Richard

GUIDE

TO

BUDDAHOOD

BEING A

STANDARD MANUAL OF CHINESE BUDDHISM

Translated by

REV. TIMOTHY RICHARD, LITT. D.

MEMBER OF THE ENGLISH BAPTIST MISSION; SECRETARY OF THE CHRISTIAN LITERATURE SOCIETY; CO-CHANCELLOR OF THE SHANSI IMPERIAL UNIVERSITY WITH THE GOVERNOR OF THE PROVINCE.

Shanghai

CHRISTIAN LITERATURE SOCIETY

1907

PRINTED BY THE SHANGHAI MERCURY, LIMITED

THE STRENGTH AND WEAKNESS
OF
ORDINARY BUDDHISM

The Strength lies in its systematic arrangement of a complete view of the universe, its aim to remove the suffering of all living beings by Ethics and by Union with the Supreme Divine Will which rules all.

The Weakness lies in its inditement of the sexual element in the universe and its vain efforts to stamp it out; its countless imaginary worlds and its imaginary beings inhabiting each, its neglecting in China, where most of the Buddhists of the world are, to take part in the practical improvement of the material, social, educational and political conditions of men regarding all such things as compared with the eternal, nothing but vanity!

T. R.

TRANSLATOR'S PREFACE.

DR. Eitel's "Three Lectures on Buddhism" and his "Sanscrit-Chinese and English Dictionary" are amongst the very best authorities on Buddhism in China but it was most unfortunate to have called his splendid Dictionary a "Hand-book on Buddhism" for you might as consistently call a standard English Dictionary a Hand-book of Christian Civilization! But this book and Dr. Eitel's Dictionary fit each other like a lock and its key.

Now in this "Guide to Buddhahood" which the Chinese call *Hsuan Fo P'u* 選佛譜 you will actually get Buddhism arranged in a definite and regular order, beginning with the lowest scale of existence and ascending regularly through the different stages of progress till finally Paradise and Buddhahood are attained, and thus you find this book a true Hand-book of Buddhism—a sort of counterpart to the Dictionary, as the chapters and sub-divisions are arranged in a logical instead of an Alphabetical order.

I have read all the books of any note written in the English language on Buddhism, but I have never read any which gives a more complete view of Buddhism as I have found it in China than is given in this little book.

I translated it about ten years ago, avoiding only the detailed and rather tedious explanations of many of the sub-divisions. I had hoped to have leisure to revise it, but as increasing duties seem to put off that leisure indefinitely, and as many might be glad to have this outline of Buddhism as written by the Chinese themselves, I submit it, notwithstanding its imperfections, to those who wish to study Buddhism as found in China.

TRANSLATOR'S INTRODUCTION.

BUDDHIST STANDARD BOOKS.

CHINESE Buddhism has three books which stand out pre-eminently among the rest, viz., the philosophic book called *The Awakening of Faith* 大乘起信論 translated into Chinese which is acknowledged to be the fountain from which modern Buddhism of the Far East arose, the popular book which might be termed the *Buddhist Pilgrim's Progress* though the Chinese name of it is the Sacred book of the Goddess of Mercy, 觀音濟度本願眞經 and the *Guide to Buddhahood* which is here translated and which gives a bird's eye view of the whole of Buddhism and the stages of progress in Buddhist learning from the lowest to the highest rung in the ladder, and in the various schools of Buddhism.

OLD AND NEW BUDDHISM.

As the Christians have their Old and New Testament so have Buddhists their Old and New Form which differ as much from one another as Christianity differs from the Jewish religion with its repulsive slaughter houses in the tabernacle and temple. The Hindu names for these two forms are the Hinayana and the Mabayana—the elementary and the advanced.

The former gives primitive atheistic views and the brotherhood of man in contrast with the polytheism and the caste system of Brahmanism but it practically failed to be acceptable to Mongolia and China. About the beginning of the Christian era, Buddhism underwent a grat change which was called the Advanced Buddhism with Amitabha, the God of endless age, at its root and became acceptable to all the nations of the Far East.

Confusion from not Knowing the Difference.

Some eminent writers on Buddhism like Oldenberg thinking that the only way to get at Buddhism proper was by studying the documents of the primitive Hinayana school which is like a man trying to understand Christianity by the study of the Old Testament only, while others like Sir Edwin Arnold finding in the Mahayana school much that was similar to Christianity jumped to the conclusion that that was Buddhism which he called the *Light of Asia* with the result that the readers of Buddhist literature in the West are bewildered by inexplicable contradictions not knowing that the essentials of the Mahayana school were mainly from the same source as Christianity. That foreigners should be bewildered by this is no wonder for the best students of Buddhism in the Far East themselves declare that it is impossible to reconcile the two and they therefore call the Mahayana form the New Religion or New Buddhism. This matter is fully discussed in the Introduction to the Author's translation of the *Awakening of Faith* published in Shanghai.

Some Account of this Book.

The Chinese copy of this book was originally published in A.D. 1593 and is now republished in two vols. at Hangchow, Soochow and Nanking. It is based on a previous smaller and imperfect book called *Shing* Fo *Too* 升佛圖 on the model of an official book called *Shing Kwan Too* 升官圖 by which the various steps in the promotion and degradation of all classes of officials are made familiar. But the book is full of repetitions meant for thoroughly grounding beginners just as there are recapitulations and questions in textbooks for beginners in the West. As the readers of this book in English will not be tyros in study I have therefore thought it best to avoid the repetitions and even some unrepeated details and to give the gist of the whole book in as brief a manner as clearness of illustration will permit, only giving in full some parts which are peculiar in order to give a fair view of the whole.

The technical terms are given in Chinese as well as in English as they will be found useful in the study of other Buddhist literature in the Chinese language.

I made the translation in 1895 and hoped to have time to revise it before publication but as I see no prospect of getting such a time I publish it in the hope that it will save the students of Chinese Buddhism much time and labour.

The Awakening of Faith and this *Guide to Buddhahood* form a sort of Alpha and Omega of Chinese Buddhism. They are far more comprehensive and complete on their lines than anything published in English. From these both the stren and weakness of Buddhism may be easily seen.

Shanghai, March 1907.

TIMOTHY RICHARD.

GUIDE TO BUDDHAHOOD.

CONTENTS.

TRANSLATOR'S SYNOPSIS.

AUTHOR'S INTRODUCTORY REMARKS.

CHAP. I.—STEPS IN THE BEGINNING OF DEPARTURE FROM EVIL. 發始因地門

1. The ten worst crimes. 上品十惡
2. The ten medium crimes. 中品十惡
3. The ten lighter crimes. 下品十惡
4. Self-will. 見取
5. Charity without love. 慢心行施
6. Conventional goodness. 世間福
7. Formalists. 戒取
8. Lowest class of worldly goodness—negative. 下品十善
9. Second class of worldly goodness—improvement. 中品十善
10. Best class of worldly goodness. 上品十善
11. Heretics missing the way. 邪定
12. Tasters of meditation. 味禪
13. Four fundamental meditations. 根本四禪
14. The four immeasurables. 四無量心
15. Meditation on the four immaterial things. 四無色定
16. Meditation on human opinions. 意見叅禪
17. Practice of religion for gain and fame. 利名習教
18. Supermundane happiness. 出世福業

19. Supermundane science of discipline.
出世戒學
20. Supermundane science of meditation.
出世定學
21. Supermundane science of wisdom.
出世慧學

CHAP. II.—STEPS IN IMPERFECT RELIGIOUS LIFE.
法道流弊門

1. Breaking of the Buddhist commandments.
破尸羅
2. Breaking the eight commandments. 破軌則
3. Bringing the truth into disrepute. 毀正見
4. Despising learning. 棄多聞
5. Growing in conceit. 增上慢

CHAP. III.—STEPS IN THE FOUR STATES OF EXISTENCE.
四種惡趣門

1. Those in the hell of longest duration.
阿鼻地獄
2. Those in the uninterrupted or common hell.
無門地獄
3. Those in the interrupted or partitioned hell.
有間地獄
4. Those in the form of the lowest animals.
下品畜生
5. Those in the form of common animals.
中品畜生
6. Those in the form of the higher animals.
上品畜生
7. Those who are beggar ghosts. 無財鬼
8. Those who are poor ghosts. 少財鬼
9. Those who are well-to-do ghosts. 有財鬼
10. Those who are animal asuras. 畜修羅

2. The 2nd Brahmaloka—Attendant Brahmas.
梵輔天
3. The 3rd Brahmaloka—Royal Brahmas.
大梵天
4. The 4th Brahmaloka. 少光天
5. The 5th Brahmaloka. 無量光天
6. The 6th Brahmaloka. 光音天
7. The 7th Brahmaloka. 少淨天
8. The 8th Brahmaloka. 無量淨天
9. The 9th Brahmaloka. 徧淨天
10. The 10th Brahmaloka. 福生天
11. The 11th Brahmaloka. 福愛天
12. The 12th Brahmaloka. 廣果天
13. The 13th Brahmaloka. 無想天
14. The 14th Brahmaloka. 無煩天
15. The 15th Brahmaloka. 無熱天
16. The 16th Brahmaloka. 善見天
17. The 17th Brahmaloka. 善現天
18. The 18th Brahmaloka. 色究景天

B. THE IMMATERIAL REALM.

19. The 1st immaterial heaven—of boundless space. 空無邊處天
20. The 2nd immaterial heaven—of boundless knowledge. 識無邊處天
21. The 3rd immaterial heaven—of absolutely no place. 無所有處天
22. The 4th immaterial world—of neither thought nor no-thought. 非想非非想處天
23. The state of the bare Arhat. 鈍根阿那含

CHAP. VI.—THE STEPS IN DOING GOOD AND SUPPRESSING EVIL. 生善滅惡門

1. Making all kinds of beings to hear Buddha's doctrine. 聽法雜衆

5. Reflection on the eight beliefs. 八念觀
6. Reflection on the ten thoughts. 十想觀
7. Eight mortifications. 八背捨
8. Reflection on the eight victories. 八勝處觀
9. Reflection on the ten abstract ideas. 十一切處觀
10. Contemplation on the nine steps. 九次第定
11. The Master's quick joy. 師子奮迅三昧
12. The joy that is surpassing. 超越三昧
13. The joy that is royal or supreme. 王三昧

CHAP. IX.—THE STEPS IN THE GROWTH OF WISDOM. 增上慧學門

1. Learn the Law. 發聲聞心
2. Learn to be an ascetic. [the 12 nidanas] 發辟支佛心
3. Serve the six ways of salvation [Paramita] also the four truths. 事六度心
4. Body forth reflections on the immaterial. 體空觀
5. Three reflections in order. 次第三觀
6. Reflection on the Mysterious Perfect Efficiency or Mainspring. 圓頓妙觀
7. Desire to ascend to the Mansion of Maitreya. 願升內院
8. Seek to get to the Pure Land. 求生淨土

CHAP. X.—THE STEPS IN THE ORIGINAL [HINAYANA] SCHOOL. 藏敎位次門

1. The stage of the five heart rests. 五停心
2. The stage of thinking of another state. 別相念

3. The stage of thinking of the general state.
   總相念
4. Hot zeal stage. 煖位
5. Mountain—top stage. 頂位
6. The stage of perseverance. 忍位
7. The highest stage in this world. 世第一位
8. The first degree of graduation.
   初果須陀洹
9. The second degree. 二果斯陀含
10. The third degree [Anajamin]. 三果阿那含
11. The fourth degree [Arhat]. 四果阿羅漢
12. The Pratycka Buddha degree.
    中乘辟支佛果
13. 1st degree of the Mahayana School.
    大乘初阿僧祇滿
14. 2nd degree of the Mahayana School.
    二阿僧祇滿
15. 3rd degree of the Mahayana School.
    三阿僧祇滿
16. Buddaship of the Orthodox or Hinayana School. 藏教佛果

Chapter. XI.—The steps of the Broad School.
通教位次門

1. Stage of heavenly wisdom. 乾慧地
2. Stage of the spiritual nature. 性地
3. Stage of the eight endurances. 八人地
4. Stage of sight. 見地
5. The thin stage. 薄地
6. The stage free from desire. 離欲地
7. The stage of finished work. 已辨地

8. The Pratyeka Buddha state [See chap X. 12]. 辟支佛地
9. The Buddhisatwa state [Pusaship chap IV. 14]. 菩薩地
10. The Buddhas state [Mahayana]. 佛地

Chapter. XII.—The steps of the New School [Mahayana]. 別教位次門

1–10. The ten aims or ten faiths [chap XIII. 2]. 十心:—

1. To have Faith. 信心
2. To be thoughtful. 念心
3. To Progress. 精進心
4. To have Wisdom. 慧心
5. To Contemplate. 定心
6. To Persevere. 不退心
7. To Defend the doctrine. 護法心
8. To return to the cause of things. 迴向心
9. To have self control. 戒心
10. To have a desire to save others. 願心

11-20. The ten grades. 十住:—

11. The purpose grade. 初發心住
12. The grade discipline. 治地住
13. The grade of religious practice. 修行住
14. The grade of noble birth. 生貴住
15. The grade of perfect means. 方便具足住
16. The grade of right mind. 正心住
17. Standing grade. 不退住
18. Grade of immortal youth. 童眞住
19. Grade of heirs of the king of law. 法王子住
20. Ordained grade. 灌頂住

21-30. The ten characteristics 十行:—

21. Joyous. 歡喜行
22. Forgiving. 饒益行
23. Without hate. 無嗔恨行
24. Inexhaustible. 無盡行
25. Without fanaticism. 離痴亂行
26. Influential. 善現行
27. Quiet. 無著行
28. Honourable. 尊重行
29. Organizing. 善法行
30. True. 眞實行

31-40. The ten returns 十廻向:—

31. To the saving of all from the present state.
救護衆生離衆生相廻向
32. To the indestructible. 不壞廻向
33. To equality with Buddhas. 等一切佛廻向
34. To the omnipresent. 至一切處廻向
35. To inexhaustible treasures. 無盡功德藏廻向
36. To obedience of eternal goodness.
隨順平等善根廻向
37. To obedience of eternal reflection.
隨順等觀一切衆生廻向
38. To the Architype. 眞如相廻向
39. To deliverance from bondage.
無縛解脫廻向
40. To the infinite eternal realm.
法界無量廻向

41-50. The ten attainments 十地:—

41. The Peaceful. 歡喜地
42. The Holy. 離垢地
43. The Enlightening. 發光地
44. The Burning with wisdom. 燄慧地

45. The Surpassing. 難勝地
46. The All-pervading. 現前地
47. The Far-reaching. 遠行地
48. The Calm. 不動地
49. The Graciously wise. 善慧地
50. The Celestial. 法雲地
51. The universal enlightenment (Buddhisatwa-Pusaship). 等覺菩薩
52. The mysterious enlightenment of Buddhas according to the Mahayana school. 別教妙覺佛位

CHAP. XIII.—THE STEPS OF THE COMPLETE SCHOOL. 圓教位次門

1. The place of the five arts. 圓五品位
2. The place of the ten faiths. 圓十信位
3. The place of the ten grades. 圓十住位
4. The place of the ten characterists. 圓十行位
5. The place of the ten returns. 圓十廻向位
6. The place of the ten attainments. 圓十地位
7. The place of the universal enlightenment. 圓等覺位
8. The place of the pure diamond. 金剛後心

CHAP. XIV.—THE STEPS IN THE PURE [CROSS-PASSAGE] SCHOOL. 淨土橫超門

1. The Doubting City of the Pure Land. 淨土疑城
2. The lowest class in the elementary stage. 下品下生
3. The intermediate class in the elementary stage. 下品中生

4. The highest class in the elementary stage.
下品上生
5. The lowest class in the intermediate stage.
中品下生
6. The intermediate class in the intermediate stage. 中品中生
7. The highest class in the intermediate stage.
中品上生
8. The lowest class in the advanced stage.
上品下生
9. The intermediate class in the advanced stage.
上品中生
10. The highest class in the advanced stage.
上品上生
11. The Pure Land of abounding goodness.
方便有餘淨土
12. The Pure Land of glorious real recompense.
實報莊嚴淨土
13. The Pure Land of Eternal Calm Light.
常寂光淨土

CHAP. XV.—THE HIGHEST RESULT OF ALL THE SCHOOLS—BUDDHAHOOD! 圓極果位門

AUTHOR'S INTRODUCTORY REMARKS.

What the Characters on the Dice Indicate.

In order thoroughly to learn the steps of progress in Buddhist life from beginning to end there is a game made of it with the six syllables Na Mo O Mi To Fo, one on each side of a cube dice. The two syllables Na mo represent evil; the four syllables O mi to fo represent good.

1. Na indicates care, departure from truth and doubt.
2. Mo indicates fondness for the cares of the world, called also doubts and prejudices and also what their end will come to.
3. O indicates charity.
4. Mi indicates morality
5. To indicates contemplation.
6. Fo indicates wisdom.

Again.

O indicates the state of birth and death i.e. mortality.

Mi indicates the state of no birth or death i.e. immortality.

To indicates the state of gradual attainment of religion.

Fo indicates the state of perfect immediate attainment of it.

To those who ask why we use these six syllables instead of the numbers 1, 2, 3, 4, 5, 6, it is answered that mere numbers cannot stop evil or produce good; it is because these sacred syllables are the names for all virtue. By hearing the name of Buddha man may attain to the highest possible enlightenment, and by calling upon Buddha he can put an end to the million sins of the mortal life. When one thought corresponds to the eternal thought that thought is the same as Buddha's; when every thought corresponds to the eternal then every thought is like Buddha's, therefore we have used these six syllables for our game.

Namo is a word meaning Return to obedience. As to the three classes the One Soul Buddha and "all living beings"— are originally of one nature there should not be any difference or distinction of good and evil among one class more than the other, and therefore how can one class be spoken of as repenting more than another? Yet as some have got entangled in mortal existence we talk of those awaking as a class of "all beings" returning. The Buddhas are those who have returned. As those who have returned should body forth this goodness, and this bodying forth is because they have returned, should we then not indicate their whole course on their returning path?

The game begins with Namo indicating evil, the greatest evils first and ascending to the lighter ones afterwards. The four syllables O mi to fo indicate Charity, morality, contemplation and knowledge, all of which are contained in the Scriptures of both of the Smaller and the Larger schools [Hinayana and the Mahayana].

When these four chief virtues are observed the other virtues of patience and perseverance in the Six Paths of Salvation are included and even the last four of the Ten Paths of salvation, viz. 7th Right Means, 8th Vows, 9th Force of Purpose, 10th Wisdom.

There is also a division into the perfect and the imperfect goodness. When charity, morality and contemplation have nothing in them superior to worldly wisdom they are termed finite. But true wisdom is called the infinite goodness. And if charity, morality and contemplation are guided by infinite wisdom they also may be termed infinite. By worldly knowledge we mean that which does not penetrate into the real essence of infinite truth (Pradjna) only knowing finite virtue and happiness.

Lastly, finite wisdom is shown in four stages:—

The rudimentary stage of the three schools.

The intelligent stage of the three schools.

The rudimentary stage of the higher school.

The intelligent stage of the higher school.

GUIDE TO BUDDHAHOOD.

CHAPTER I.

The steps in the stage of beginning and growth of character. 發始因地門

1. 上品十惡 We begin with all (10) worst crimes. Those who not only commit all (10) crimes but do so with aggravations. The 10 crimes are 1. to kill, 2. to steal, 3. to commit adultery, 4. to bear false witness, 5. to be double-faced, 6. to curse, 7. to speak vain words, 8. to covet, 9. to be angry, 10. to be wrong religiously (heterodox).

When these ten crimes are aggravated, such as when parents, teachers or Buddhist monks are killed, when things belonging to the Three Precious Ones [the Eternal, the Law and the Priesthood] are stolen, and when crimes of impurity are committed against the pure and against near relations, and when the prince, parents, teachers and saviours are despised and insulted with extra passion, and when these crimes are repeated incessantly without repentance— this is the way to Hell. But if people repent of these and obtain the help of Buddha, then according to their diligence in the good way they may only be sent to the Hell of incessant pain for one great kalpa, or to the hell of occasional respite from punishment, or to bare existence on earth, (See I. 6) or may hear the Law, may make confession to the Brothers, or finally attain to the lowest grade of the third degree in the Pure Land. [See Chap. XIV.2]

2. 中品十惡 Those who commit all [10] crimes of a slighter degree. Crimes committed against the life of men and devas, against the property of men and devas but not aggravated with extreme passion. The recompense of such crimes is to be born in the animal kingdom. The lowest of this class will appear as gnats, blue-flies, mole-crickets, ants etc. Less evil ones as birds, cows, horses, while those of this class who have done any good however small will appear as unicorns, phoenixes, dragons, elephants, lions, Chinese roc-birds.

But if they give up evil and begin to do a little good, learn wisdom and depend on Buddha's power then they may ascend from being born among the lowest animals into the second grade of animals, or into the highest grade of animals, or ascend into the rank of animal Asuras, (III 10-13) or hearers of the law, or among the second class of penitents (Chap. VI. 5) or the highest class of penitents or even the second grade of the lowest degree in the Pure Land. (XIV. 3)

3. 下品十惡 Those who commit crimes of the lightest degree; such as killing, stealing etc. committed against hungry spirits but with passing passions. The recompense for this is to become hungry ghosts. But by learning to do good and by dependence on Buddha's strength these may rise from being the poorest hungry ghosts possessing nothing, to be poor ghosts who have a little of their own, or to be ghosts who have much possession, or to be penitents of the third class (Chap. VII. 1, 2)

4. 見取 Those who are opinionative trusting to their own experience and ignoring others. The asuras of men and devas come from these. (Chap. III. 12, 13)

5. 慢心行施 Those who give charity in a proud manner. These do not go to hell but are sowing the seed for becoming asuras in the future.

6. 世福間 Those who are good in the estimation of the world. Generally speaking those who practise charity, discipline and contemplation.

7. 戒取 Those who are formalists. Those who follow all sorts of observances, such as the cow and the dog prohibition, prohibition about ashes, pulling hairs, branding the body, fastings, etc. These may become wheel princes (kings). (Chap. IV. 5. 8)

8. 下品十善 Those who do the lowest grade of good deeds—negative goodness, such as (1) not to kill, (2) not to steal, (3) not to commit adultery, (4) not to speak falsely, (5) not to be double-faced, (6) not to be evil-tongued, (7) not to speak vanity (8) not to covet, (9) not to be angry, (10) not to be heretical.

9. 中品十善 Those who practise the second grade of good deeds. That is when the lowest grade of good deeds are done well, or often, or occasionally with zeal.

10. 上品十善 Those who practice the best kind of good deeds; they do the above good deeds very zealously or perform them on a large scale or for a long time, but still they practise only miscellaneous goodness, therefore they are to be rewarded only in the world of desire in heaven. (Chap. IV)

11. 邪定 Those who follow after religion though heretical. This is when all learning is studied from a false point of view such as the 95 strange religions of the West, and the religions of those who worship foxes (sort of fairies) and animals, ghosts and spirits.

12. 味禪 Those who begin tasting contemplation. In the four contemplations there are in each three different kinds, viz. that which corresponds to that of the delivered, called the first of the perfect contemplation; that which corresponds to the five branches, (Chap. I. 13) and the four branches of merit, it is called the first of the pure contemplation; that which corresponds to each of the trials of life is called the beginning of tasting contemplation.

13. 根本四禪 Those of the four fundamental contemplations. There are the four contemplations, the four contemplations of the four immeasurables, (Chap. I. 14) and contemplations of the four unseen; (Chap. I. 15), in all twelve kinds of contemplations, called also the pure contemplations of this world. Beginning with the four fundamental contem-

plations, these have each special means of their own. First we discuss contemplation of the visible world. It commences when a man sits cross-legged to exercise the breath, beginning roughly proceeding gently in harmony with the physical nature. After which the body and mind fall into a trance and lose consciousness, and while sitting thus are unconscious of head or body, just as like empty space. This is the preparatory contemplation, or first meditation. This is the first exercise. It is also called the coming contemplation. It is to be done without fear and without joy, for both fear and joy may call up a demon, and without speaking, (to speak is to break the spell and may never get it again), like transplanting a tree the root must be taken up. By entering the contemplation through the preparatory stage gradually the mind and body become as nothing, unconscious of anything inward or outward, passing a day or a week or even a year in incessant meditation, defending the doctrine and growing in knowledge till suddenly one will feel a spasm going through the mind and body. Consciousness gradually returns like a cloud or a shadow passing from the upper or from the lower part of the body, or from the waist, spreading over the whole body. At this time the good gained is incalculable. 1. one is grounded, 2. the ideal is set up, 3. purity is understood, 4. there is joy, 5. there is gladness, 6. goodness is begotten, 7. one discovers what knowledge is, 8. there is deliverance from hindrances, 9. the final good appears, 10. there is a tender heart. Such are ten spiritual blessings, and glories of this stage.

Now we proceed to consider in brief detail this first stage whether it lasts for a day, or ten days, or a month or four months or even a year. In the first contemplation certain sensations regularly appear, though not necessarily in the same order. The sensations are first the above spasm of the body, 2. feeling of itchiness. 3. of cold, 4 of heat, 5 of lightness, 6 of heaviness, 7 of roughness, 8 of smoothness. And there are other 8 sensations, such as, 1 of falling, 2 of leaning on something, 3 of cold 4 of heat, 5 of floating, 6 of sinking in water, 7 of strenght, 8 of weakness. These eight though similar to the first eight are really somewhat different. These sixteen sensations arise together and have ten different benefits. As these sensations and benefits are experienced before one really gets fully grounded, this stage is called the beginning of the first contemplation.

Men depend on the four pure elements [earth, water, fire and wind] and on the senses. Here one leaves the five senses and the five emotions. The five desires are—form, sound, scent, taste and touch. The five emotions are—anger, desire, sleep, recklessness, doubt, and secure the five branches of blessings of the first contemplation, viz. enlightenment, reflection, joy, pleasure and the realization of the one soul within.

If one succeeds with the first contemplation neither losing nor falling back in it, then there will be life in the end according to the degree of thoroughness of the first contemplation will certainly be born in the three mansions of the Brahman subjects. [Chap. V. 1.] Thus is the seed of heaven sown in the first contemplation.

[2] The second contemplation is when one leaves the state of the senses and reflection and enters on a higher meditation. If one sets his mind on it incessantly afterwards, all things will suddenly become perfectly clear and he will be filled with rest and joy and the four branches of blessings, such as [1] inward purity, [2] joy, [3] gladness, [4] the indwelling of the One Soul]. This is called the second meditation of the fundamentals. When a man follows this course he will in the end according to his attainments be born in the mansion of limited light. [Chap. V. 4] Thus is the seed of Heaven sown in the second meditation.

[3] The third contemplation is when one leaves the state of joy and enters on a higher meditation. If one continues from the beginning pleasing his heart and seeking rest as naturally as if going to sleep, not depending on anything inward or outward, then gladness springs up in his heart, full of the five blessing [such as 1. disinterestedness, 2. thoughtfulness, 3, wisdom, 4. gladness, 5. the indwelling of the One-Soul]. When a man follows this course he will in the end be born according to his attainments in the mansions of limited purity. This is the seed of Heaven sown in the third meditation.

[4] The fourth contemplation is when one leaves the state of gladness and deeply sees the sins and

sorrows of life and still enters on a higher meditation so as to be unmoved. After this the mind suddenly opens out and is now at rest with every hindrance cut off and full of four blessings [such as 1. perfect peace, neither joy nor sorrow, 2. disinterestedness, 3. pure thought, 4. union with the One-Soul]. When a man follows this he is certain to be born in heaven in the mansion of happy birth. This is the seed of heaven sown in the fourth meditation.

Those who have practised the four contemplations have subdued the senses and the affections.

14. 四無量心 Contemplation of four boundless virtues. They are also called the four divine-like virtues. They are love pity, joy and self-sacrifice. The practice of these come after the four meditations. [1] Boundless love loves all living beings and rejoices to forgive and do them good. [2] Boundless pity pities all suffering beings in the five ways of existence. [3] Boundless joy desires to lead all beings from pleasure to joy. [4] Boundless self-sacrifice which contemplates all living beings without passion. Those who practise these well will finally be born in heaven as Princes of the four meditations, therefore those who practise the four boundless virtues are free from the punishments due to evil.

15. 四無色定 The four Contemplations on the immaterial.

[1] On space. Those who do so properly will not fail to be born in the Mansion of Boundless Space. [Chap. V. 19]

[2] On knowledge of time, past, present and to come. Those who do so properly will not fail to be born in the Mansion of Boundless Knowledge. [Chap. V. 20]

[3] On State of being. (Non-localization.) Those who properly do so will not fail to be born in the Mansion of Non-localization. [Chap. V. 21]

[4] On No-care. Those who properly do so will be born in the Mansion of No-care. [Chap. V. 22].

16. 意見叅禪 Contemplation of the mental realm. This is the study of super-mundane wisdom with the object of discovering the original Soul behind all things. It is the same as the meditation of the Complete and of the Sudden School.

17. 利名習教 Practice of religion by those fond of gain and fame. They learn supermundane wisdom and thus transmit this wisdom and life of Buddha for him.

18. 出世福業 The business of super-mundane happiness. Those who practise the five Paramita virtues of charity, morality, patience, progress and meditation, are called those who are adorned with super-mundane happiness. At present men first keep the Buddhist commandments and then read some literature to understand and contribute something in charity to secure happiness and be delivered from the rounds of life and death. This is called the business of super-mundane happiness. They start with the

happiness of the three Precious Ones—[the principal gods in the Buddhist temples representing Buddha, the Law, and the Church]

19. 出世戒學 Supermundane discipline [laws]. There are two kinds, one for laymen at home and five kinds for monks who have left their home, making seven kinds in all, both in the shorter (Hinayana) and the larger (Mahayana) school. These are what we call superhuman laws. The lay laws for men and women of the primary class are the five commandments (Chap. VII 1.) which are observed throughout life. The laws for the other lay class of upasakas, male and female, called the pure life disciples, are the eight commandments [Chap. VII 2.] which they observe on fast days.

As to demons, animals and evil men, they cannot observe the five commandments. They can only keep them for one day and night during the six fasting days and plant some seeds of better life hereafter. Therefore instead of the eight commandments they should begin with the five. As these cannot observe the important rules and are only just able to join those who have left the world, (i.e. enter the monastery), they themselves cannot be called those who have left the world. Now beginners start with the five commandments. Secondly, after a year and three months they begin to observe the eight commandments. Thirdly, they leave home as monks and nuns and observe the ten commandments. Fourthly, they observe the rules of a bhikshu [Chap. VII.] and enter the rank of the great monks [mendicants]. Fifthly, they observe also the rules for the female mendicants. [Bhikshuni] This is called observing the commandments of the two classes of discipline. Sixthly, they know and observe widely and thoroughly the common laws of Buddhism. Seventhly, they get the perfect and divine discipline and put off for ever the desire to break these laws; this is called abiding in the law—the holy state. Eighthly, those who can be without family ties or care who have no fear or anxiety and who possess great virtue and ability and have the power to govern others.

The above include the seven classes of the Shorter course, [Hinayana school]. Those of the five commandments include the two lay classes at home [Yuposai, Yupoi] who only keep the commandments for one day and night [fast days].

Those of the ten commandments include three classes who have left their homes, viz. Shichamona, Shami and Shamini.

Those who observe the five disciplines of the smaller Bhikshus and Bhikshuni (mendicants) making 7 classes in all.

20. 出世定學 Supermundane Contemplations. Generally speaking these are four.

The first is the mundane meditation called the four meditations [Chap. I. 13.] the four Divine Virtues. [Chap. I. 14.] the four immaterials [Chap. I. 15.] already explained.

The second is partly mundane and partly supermundane, called the six divine gates and the sixteen victories.

The third is supermundane and called the four ways of reflection, purification influence and practice.

The fourth is neither mundane nor supermundane but the peace of the Middle or Broad School.

21. 出世慧學 Supermundane wisdom. This embraces the four axiomatic truths of Buddhism, the doctrine of Karma [?] the [six or ten] paths of salvation and reflection.

CHAPTER II.

THE STEPS IN THE IMPERFECT CHARACTER OF THE RELIGIOUS. 法道流弊門

1. 破尸羅 The breaking of the Buddhist commandments i.e. The seven commandments common to the Hinayana and Mahayana schools.

2. 破軌則 Breaking the eight commandments, (Chap. VII 1. 2.) ? such as the 8 rules for the lay members, and Buddhist proprieties, which are that men should live in poor houses on poor fare ; not to dig the earth or injure anything that grows—like trees and flowers ; nor put gold or silver ornaments on animals, etc.

3. 毀正見 Bringing the truth into disrepute by trusting in one's own power to understand the highest mysteries and not believing in Yu lai's word, sometimes talking recklessly about the Law and the Unseen, at other times holding only one school of thought important, or despising rules as of small consequence, or regarding Sacred books as mere exhortations ; all this is bringing the truth into disrepute.

4. 棄多聞 Despising learning.

Increase of learning makes increase of true wisdom, therefore the Bodhisatvas constantly rejoice in increasing their knowledge and learning.

5. 增上慢 Growing in conceit.

CHAPTER III.

STEPS IN THE FOUR EVIL STATES.
四種惡趣門

According to some there are six classes of Beings—three evil ones, such as those in hell, animals, and hungry ghosts (Pretas), and three better ones such as devas, men and asuras; according to others there are only five, the asuras being included among the devas. Although there is some good in them they are generally full of trickery, therefore often classed with the three evil classes making four.

1. 阿鼻地獄 Those in the hell, of longest duration [Avitchi], who are entirely evil and have no good in them, are placed in the midst of suffering out of which it is difficult to escape.

2. 無門地獄 Those in the "uninterrupted" or common hell who are also entirely evil and are placed there for a long period during which they cannot harbour doubts.

3. 有間地獄 Those in the interrupted or partitioned hell who are 90 per cent thoughtless, who are recompensed according to their deeds without any fixed period of time.

4. 下品畜生 Those who are in the lowest forms of animals—small and ugly, in darkness, having only pain and no pleasure.

5. 中品畜生 Those who are in the common forms of animals, such as birds, beasts on land or in the water, feathered or scaly, ugly or stinking, whether preying on one another or are serving as slaves.

6. 上品畜生 Those who are in the higher forms of animals, such as royal dragons, royal elephants, royal golden-winged birds, royal lions, etc.

7. 無財鬼 Those who are begging ghosts with evil, weak forms who have nothing but trouble without any pleasure.

8. 少財鬼 Those poor ghosts with ugly forms which find their food with much trouble; have little pleasure and much pain.

9. 有財鬼 Those who are well-to-do ghosts. Although they have ugly forms still they are receiving considerable reward for the good they have done in a former existence.

10. 畜修羅 Those who are animal asuras whose abode is in the depth of the ocean and deep sea caverns which go out in the morning into the air but return at night to the waters. They are begotten in the water.

11. 鬼修羅 Those who are demon asuras. They are oviparous; they are able to appear in the sky in defence of the Law.

12. 人修羅 Those who are human asuras who have fallen from virtue in heaven and reside near the sun and moon. These belong to the order of mamalia.

13. 天修羅 Those who are deva asuras. There is the king of all asuras who rules the whole world, most powerful and fearless, ready to oppose even Brahma and Indra.

CHAPTER IV.

STEPS IN THE REALM OF DESIRE, [KAMADHATU]. 欲界人天門.

This includes the four continents, the four wheels and ten genii, all belonging to men, the four kings even to the mansions where the free devas live [par. 17] which are called the six devalokas. Men, devas, asuras, ghosts and animals all require food and sleep and are male and female. All enjoy colour, sound, fragrance, relish and touch, hence they are called the realm of desire [and therefore subject to metempsychosis].

As to rewards the northern continent is the best and the southern is the worst, but as to religious life the southern is best and the northern is worst. We follow the order of religious life. Although the ten genii are not in this world still they are not beyond the reach of men [par. 10]. The heirs of light [par. 14] and of the inner palace [par. 15] are all in the Tuchita mansions [par 13]. Although the devils have separate mansions they are still in the realm of desire included under the control of the three devas [par. 17].

1. 北俱盧洲 The northern victory continent is the best of the four where the residents live 1,000 years without any dying young, where there is no private property, where the ten crimes are not committed. Those of this continent are most difficult to convert and are put here as one of the eight places of correction. In the end they shall be born in heaven where there is perfect pleasure without pain and without fear of death.

2. 西牛賀洲 The Western Bull-producing continent—where the residents live 500 years but some die earlier. Hence there is care.

3. 東勝神洲 The Eastern victory continent—where the residents live 250 years but some die earlier. Hence also there is care.

4. 南贍部洲 The Southern Iron-tree continent. This is so called because there is in it a tree hard as iron. There is no fixed limit to life here, it ranges from endless years to under 10 years. It is in some respects inferior to the other continents, but it has three things superior to them, viz. the residents can stop the lust of the flesh, they have power of thought and have perseverance, therefore all the Buddhas come out of this continent. All in this continent are earnest.

5. 鐵輪王 The Iron-wheel king who rules the southern hard-tree continent by means of the ten virtues.

6. 銅輪王 The Brass-wheel king. He rules over the two continents—Southern and Eastern—also by means of the ten virtues, but superior to the iron-wheel king.

7. 銀輪王 The Silver-wheel king. He rules over three continents—the Southern, Eastern and Western—also by means of his 10 virtues, but he is superior to the Brass-wheel king.

8. 金輪王 The Gold-wheel king. He rules over the four great continents and is able to cause all under him to observe the 10 virtues, therefore he is superior to the Silver-wheel king.

9. 十種仙 The ten genii. These are those who do not follow orthodox doctrines to get peace, but follow human learning, escape human life and enter the mountains and forests. The ten kinds are the following :—

[1] Those most careful about food called earth genii.

[2] Those most careful about herbs called flying genii.

[3] Those most careful about minerals called travelling genii.

[4] Those most careful about breath called air genii.

[5] Those most careful about their "spirits" called heaven genii.

[6] Those most careful about seed called thorough-going genii.

[7] Those most careful about spells called religious genii.

[8] Those most careful about thought called shining genii.

[9] Those most careful about sexual relations called seed genii.

[10] Those most careful about transformations called surpassing genii.

These do not purify their minds according to the truth but according to some other principle. They live a thousand years far away in some mountain or on an island not near any human creature; but it is all in vain, they do not obtain the true peace. The end of all is that they have to go over the whole round of life again.

10. 四天王 The First Devaloka [Tchatur maharadja] called in Chinese Sz Wang Tien or the four royal heavens. At a distance of 40.000 yu-seuen [40 li makes one yu-seuen and 3 li one mile] from the earth in the waist of Sumeru mountain, on the top of the seven golden mountains even with the height of sun and moon there are the four royal realms, viz. that on the east, where a king rules over all the gandharvas, [beings superior to men who live on incense]; that on the south, where the growing king rules over all Kumbhandas [beings who have scrotums as large as pumpkins]; that on the south-west, where the well-informed king rules over all dragons; that on the north where the learned king rules over all yakchas. Together they control all spirits [kwei

shin] so that they dare not do mischief as they please, hence these four kings are called "the guardians of the world".

11. 忉利天 The second devaloka [Traiyastrinsas] called in Chinese Tao li tien or the 33 heavens. At the top of Sumeru mountain [Su mi shan] 80,000 yu-seuen [i.e. 3,200,000 li] from the world where men live. On each of the four sides are 8 heavens making 32, and a central one where dwells the lord of all these heavens [Sakra, i.e. Ti Shi Tien wang], making 33 mansions in all. Those here were those who practised the 10 highest kinds of virtue. Their bodies are 1500 feet high, but the body of Sakra is 3000 feet high and 100 years of human life is only one day of his, and he lives 1000 years [i.e. 36,000,000 of our years!]

12. 夜摩天 The third devaloka [Yama] called in Chinese Yeh Mo tien or the Yama heaven. This is distant 80,000 yu-seuen [3,200,000 li] from the 33 heavens and 160,000 yu-seuen from the world of men. It is like a cloud in space. One day and night there is reckoned by the opening and closing of the lotus. Those who reach there are those who practised the ten highest virtues and also the meditations and some of the disciplines. Their bodies are 2220 feet in height and 200 years of human life are there only one day. They live there to 2000 years of their reckoning.

13. 兜率天 The fourth devaloka [Tuchita] called the Tou Swai tien by the Chinese. This is beyond the Yama heaven 160,000 yu-seuen [6,400,000 li]

and 320,000 yu-scuen from the world of men. It is like a cloud in space separated from the abodes of men and devas, different from the Yama heaven, where there are all sorts of pleasures to enjoy but yet without satisfaction. This is the result of the highest ten virtues together with and the various rules of discipline. The height of the body is 3000 feet, 400 human years are only one of their days and yet they live 4000 years of their reckoning.

14. 褮光天子 The Heirs of Light [Mêng Kwang tien 21] the Bodhisatvas in the Tuchita heaven shed a great light, hence they are called Princes of Light who shine throughout as many worlds as there are atoms in ten worlds over which Buddhas rule. [Buddha Kchetra]. When those in the hills of those worlds get any of this light all their troubles are at an end and they are filled with joy and will be born in the Tuchita heaven. In heaven there is a drum from which proceeds a voice saying "You children of heaven, as you kept your hearts from evil rooted in the root of all goodness planted in Julai, and you who have from of old kept close to all good knowledge, then by the great majestic and divine power of Vairotchana [Vairotchana is defined by Japanese Buddhist Dictionary as the omnipresent, free from all sin, perfect in all goodness, the model from whom all the Buddhas learn! you who were in the lowest hell were decreed in the end to be born in this heaven, even among the children of heaven. When the Boddhisatva Vairotchana enters the peace of purity you should reverently worship him." When the devas heard this

they all thought this is strange and extraordinary, what is the cause of this small mysterious voice. The heavenly drum says "The words which I say are caused by goodness. O ye devas, I speak of myself but it is not of self nor of my state. All Buddhas are also the same. They speak of themselves as Buddhas but are not thinking of self nor of their own state. O ye devas, if my voice does not come from the east or the south, west or north, the points of the compass, nor from above or below, then the recompense that becomes a Buddha is so also; it does not come from any outside quarter. O ye devas, suppose you were formerly in hell, hell and your body did not come from any outside quarter, only from your topsy-turvy evil ways binding you in your foolish madness, so that you had a body fit for hell. This has no other root or source but in yourselves."

"O ye devas, the Bodhisatva Vairotchana on account of the power of his great virtue sheds forth great light, but this light does not come from space. O ye devas, the voice of my heavenly drum is so also. It does not come from space but comes from the power of the goodness of peace, from the power of the great virtue of the Supreme [Paramita] Wisdom and thus produces a pure sound manifesting all kinds of wisdom, and freedom so that you should visit the place of this Bodhisatva and support him without coveting any more of the pleasures of the world. To let the pleasures of the world mar good works is like letting a stupendous fire burn the mountain of Sumeru. All of it will be burnt up. Desires in the heart are just like that, you can no longer have a desire to think of Buddha. O ye devas, you should know that Grace rewards Grace!"

Then all the devas when they heard all this were moved into ten thousand clouds of flowers and ten thousand clouds of incense going to the palace where the Bodhisatva was desiring to see them, but they heard that he had died and gone down to be born in the southern iron-tree continent among men. But there was a voice from the drum saying the Bodhisatva is not dead but appears in another world to help spiritually according to the need of all and thus make himself manifest. You should make up your mind to have "unexcelled perfect intelligence" [Anuttara samyak sambodhi], to be pure in thought, abiding in the majesty of goodness, repenting of and putting away all sins, such as those in trials, in seeking rewards, in sightseeing, and even in talking of recompense, as if those came accidentally like dreams or doubts."

When the devas had heard they had eternal divine patience. Having reached this highest [10th] stage they saw a hundred thousand times a hundred thousand of Nahutas [each of which is 100 millions] equal in number to the atoms of a whole world [Buddha Kchekra] of lotus flowers on each of which was a Bodhisatva shedding light, manifesting Buddha. Thus they extensively produced good kind deeds like flowers and incense to support them and all beings got the benefit of them and attained the highest stage [10th] of good. These also in their turn shed light and got those whom they met to attain to the highest stage of good, and thus we have what are called the three kinds of suddeners, a school of Buddhists which attain religion suddenly].

15. 彌勒内院 The inner mansion of Maitreya called by the Chinese *Meelé Yuen.* In the Tuchita heaven there is a place called the inner palace of Meelé where the Bodhisatva lives. At the end of the world none of the three calamities reach there. The Bodhisatvas who practise all the virtues, who deeply practise meditation and who desire to get here are born here at last.

16. 化樂天 The fifth devaloka [Nirmanarati] called by the Chinese *Hwa lo tien.* At a distance of 320,000 yu-seuen [12,800,000 li] from the Tuchita heaven and 640,000 yu-seuen from human habitations, there is a place in empty space like a cloud able transform itself. Those who live here are those who have practised all the highest good together with the meditations. They are 3750 feet in height; 800 years of human life is their one day; they live 8000 years of their time.

17. 他化自在天 The sixth devaloka [Paranirmita Vasavartin] called by the Chinese *Ta hwa tsz tsai tien* or free and independent heaven floating in space like a cloud at a distance of 640,000 yu-seuen [25,600,000 li] from the Hwa lo tien of transformation but 1,280,000 distant from the world where men live in this *free* heaven, because while they can transform others they themselves are free. Those living here are those who practised all the highest virtues and the

preparatory meditations. They are 4500 feet tall and 1600 years of human life make their one day, yet they live 16,000 years of their time.

18. 魔羅天 The Mansions of Mara [Molo tien]. Above the sixth heaven there are the mansions where the Maras live under the rule of the self-governing heaven. Those born here are they who, though they may practise meditation and be very learned, still, not being free from lust, are among devils, the best to be kings of the devils, the ordinary ones to be the subjects of these devil-kings and the worst to be female devils, all of whom have their followers speaking of their own as the highest religion but have got far from the Complete, the Thorough and the Nirvana doctrine.

CHAPTER V

THE STEPS IN THE VISIBLE AND INVISIBLE REALMS OF BRAHMA. 色無色天門

The various realms of matter have the five conditions of materiality, passivity. shape, change and variety. The realms of spirit have only four conditions, viz. passivity, shape, change and variety.

[Note. In the first meditation—see Chap. VIII—this is called the Happy land independent of transmigration. In the second meditation it is called the Happy land of settled life. In the third meditation it is called the Joyful land of transcendent and superhuman joy. In the fourth meditation it is called the pure land free from all care. Together they are called the Heavenly realms emptied of all these four things, hence also called the four realms of emptiness. Collectively they are therefore called the eight realms].

[The realms of matter, Sê Kiei]

1. 梵衆天 The mansions of the pure subjects [Fan ching tien], the first Brahmaloka, the Brahma Parichadyah or Assembly of the Brahmas. This is beyond the Devalokas, far from being troubled with

desires and appetites, hence called the mansion of the Pure Ones. All the four Dyanas are called Brahmas or Pure Ones. But those in the first Dyana are those who in the end of their life are born as Brahma subjects. Their life lasts through 20 small kalpas. Their bodies are a yojana in height [60 li]. [Note. These kalpas are periods during which a physical universe is formed and destroyed. The smaller kalpas are 16,800,000 years: the medium kalpas 20 times the small, i.e. 336,000,000 years; the great kalpas of 80 small or 4 medium kalpas, i.e. 1,344,000,000 years.]

2. 梵輔天 The Mansions of the Pure attendants of Brahamas [Fan chow tien], the second Brahmaloka [the Brahma Purohitas i.e. attendants of Brahma], slightly in advance of the Brahma subjects rejoicing in observing the disciplines. They live through 40 small kalpas and in height they are one yojana i.e. 4 li.

3. 大梵天 The Mansions of the Pure kings, [Ta fan tien], the third Brahmaloka [the Maha Brahmanas] where are those who are perfect in intelligence in addition to their purity and therefore rule as kings. These are those who have studied the first contemplation [Chap. I. 12-14]. They live through 60 small kalpas and they are one yojana and a half, i.e. 60 li tall.

4. 少光天 The Mansions of limited light [Siao kwang tien], the fourth Brahmaloka Parittabhas for those who have attained the second meditation

[Dhyana] where there is joy without conscious effort or study. No fire can burn that mansion. Here they live through two kalpas and are two yojanas tall i.e. 80 li.

5. 無量光天 The Mansion of unlimited light [Wu liang kwang tien], the fifth Brahmaloka Apramanabhas shedding light to all [ten] worlds as if they were all crystal. They live throughout 4 kalpas and the bodies are 4 yojanas i.e. 160 li tall.

6. 光音天 Mansion of light and sound [Kwang Yin tien], the sixth Brahmaloka Abhasvaras. Those who are profound in the second meditation [Dhyana] and in the four immeasurables [Chap. I. 14] are finally born here. This place attracts perfect light, becomes the body of religion and produces purity and infinite benefits. They live through eight great kalpas and their bodies are 8 yojanas i.e. 320 li in height.

7. 少凈天 Mansion of limited purity [Siao ching tien], the seventh Brahmaloka Parittasubhas. Those who have practised the third meditation are born here were there are no floods. They live through 16 great kalpas and their bodies are 16 yojanas i.e. 640 li in height.

8. 無量凈天 Mansion of unlimited purity [wu liang ching], the eighth Brahmaloka? Apramanasubha. Those who often practise the third meditation are born here. They live through 32 great kalpas and are 32 yojanas i.e. 1280 li tall.

9. 徧淨天 Mansion of purity everywhere [Pien ching tien], the ninth Brahmaloka? Subhakritsna. Those who practise the third meditation and the four immeasurables [Chap. I. 14] are born here. They live through 64 great kalpas and their bodies are 64 yojanas i.e. 2560 li tall.

10. 福生天 Mansion of happy birth [Fu sêng tien], the tenth Brahmaloka Punyasprasuras Akanichtha. [This and the next "heaven of happy love" Dr Eitel says were added by the Northern Buddhists; the Singalese do not have them.] Those who practise the four studies are born here. It is also called "Mansion without a cloud," and no calamities can reach this place. They live through 125 great kalpas and are 125 yojanas i.e. 5000 li in height.

11. 福愛天 Mansion of happy love [Fu 'ai tien], eleventh Brahmaloka Anabhraka. Those who often practise the four studies are born here. Age 250 great kalpas, and height 250 yojanas i.e. 1000 li.

12. 廣果天 Mansion of abundant rewards [Kwang kwo tien], the twelth Brahmaloka Vrihatphalas. Those who practise the four meditations and the four boundless hearts [Chap. I. 14] are born here. Age 500 great kalpas, and height 500 yojanas i.e. 2000 li.

13. 無想天 Mansion of "not thinking" [Wu siang tien], the thirteenth Brahmaloka [Avriha]. Men, heavenly beings, or followers of strange religions who are dissatisfied with superficial thought and

who, after frequently cultivating religion, have put away the 2nd and 3rd meditations of the world of desire, follow the 4th meditation and put away the 6th sense, thought, so that it might not be exercised as the chief thing, are said to be in the non-thought meditation. When this is mastered then they are born in the mansion of no-thought. They live 500 great kalpas and are 500 yojanas in height.

14. 無煩天 Mansion without sorrows [Wu fan tien], 14th Brahmaloka Atapa. Those who practise the fourth meditation, putting away thought, are pure in common with all, have these five mansions from which there are no rebirths to earth [14-18]. They have attained the third degree [Chap. X. 10] and the station of burning wisdom [Chap. X. 11-44], beginning with many perfect thoughts then with many imperfect thoughts, then gradually reducing them till there are first two perfect thoughts and two imperfect ones, then only one perfect and one imperfect, when the imperfect is strengthened by the perfect and enlightenment is at hand. In the end these are born in this mansion. Age 1000 kalpas, height 1000 yojanas i.e. 40,000 li.

15. 無熱天 Mansion without heat [Wu ye tien], 15th Brahmaloka Asandjni sattva. Those who practise various meditations using the three fundamental sacrifices and letting the One Infinite Mind act on the One Finite Mind by means of the three fundamental sacrifices are born here. Age 3,000 great kalpas, height 2,000 yojanas, 80,000 li.

16. 善見天 Mansion of virtuous aims [Shen kien tien], 16th Brahmaloka Sudar Sana. These aims are three, 1st those who copy the highest examples, 2nd who improve each of the last six steps of progress, and 3rd who base all on the three fundamentals of the Mind [Chap. 1. 14] [or 1. sincerity, 2 depth of conviction and 3 vow.] Such people are born here. Age 4,000 great kalpas, height 4,000 yojanas, i.e. 160,000 li.

17. 善現天 Mansion of the Beautiful [Shen hien tien], 17th Brahmaloka Sudrisas. The beautiful ones are of four [three?] kinds; 1st those who are moved to action by the highest examples, 2nd those who endeavour to improve each of the last 9 steps of progress, 3rd those who base all on the three boundless hearts are born here. [Chap. 1. 14]. Age 8,000 great kalpas, height 8,000 yojanas i.e. 320,000 li.

18. 色究竟天 Mansions of the highest beauty of the world of form [Se kieu king tien], 18th Brahmaloka Akamichtha. Those who copy the example of the very highest meditations, who improve each of the last 12 steps and who base them on the three boundless hearts are born here. Age 1600 great kalpas, height 1600 yojanas.

[The realm of Spirit or immaterialism [Wu Se kiei].

19. 空無邊處天 Mansions of boundless space [K'ing wu pien chu], Ichatur Arupa dhatu. Men and heavenly beings if in the four meditations they can only put away all thought of the five mansions [14-18] where there are no rebirths as men, and

meditate on the immaterial then they may in the end be born in this mansion. As it is immaterial we cannot speak of different directions or different regions. There only exists the sixth sense, thought, which however makes infinite space its habitation. Age here is 20,000 great kalpas, height.

20. 識無邊處天 Mansions of boundless knowledge, 2nd Immaterial heaven [see Tchatur]. Here we do not speak of a realm of desire of matter or of space. Those who only cultivate knowledge in the end reach this mansion, but it is only that 6th sense, microscopic thought, with infinite reaches which dwells there. Age 40,000 great kalpas. These govern joys of spiritual enlightenment and consider it but ordinary in them.

21. 無所有處天 Mansions of absolutely no-place [Wu so yeu chu tien], 3rd Immaterial heaven. [See Eitel's Tchatur]. Those seeking this do not think of the realm of desire of the material realm, of space or of the world of thought, but only practise absolute nowhereness and in the end reach here. Age is 60,000 great kalpas. These govern spiritual joy and call it pleasure.

22. 非想非非想處天 Mansions of neither thought nor thoughtlessness, the 4th immaterial heaven. [see Tchatur] Those seeking this do not think of the realms of desire or form or of the other three immaterial heavens, only with the infinitesimal 6th sense they reach to the realm of that which is both existent and non-existent and are born here.

Age 80,000 great kalpas. These govern spiritual joy and call it self.

23. 鈍根阿那含 The state of the bare Arhat [Tun ken Anahau] Anagamin. Those who have attained to the 4th meditation have two natures, one which rejoices in wisdom, cultivates study and attains the five pure states in which nothing troubles them and the five mansions without rebirth; and the other which rejoices in study and meditates on the four immaterial things with a view to reach the immaterial heavens. Those who rejoice in wisdom are more intelligent and quickly leave the realm of form. Those who rejoice in study are less intelligent, so they are later in reaching the immaterial realm. This embraces the four immaterial heavens beyond which nothing exists. It is not like the Pure Ones who have existence outside theirs. But though living in the immaterial heavens and differing from ordinary men and strange religions, still they are subject to transmigration, therefore it is necessary to give a different name—Anahan—to those who are never born again as men in the world and only once more as heavenly beings when they forthwith become Arhats [Lohan] and enter Nirvana. [Chap. X. 10].

CHAPTER VI

THE STEPS IN THE STAGE OF DOING GOOD AND SUPPRESSING EVIL. 生善滅惡門

Hearing the Law, guarding the Law, seeking explanation of the Law, are various methods used to lead ordinary men to become good. Private litanies, public litanies and solemn examination litany are the three litanies used to lead to putting an end to all sins which smother the Eternal Soul, and the first steps to the knowledge of Buddhism.

1. 聽法雜衆 By all kinds of beings listening to Buddha's doctrine. Those in the hell of interrupted rebirths, such as animals, hungry ghosts, asuras and bad men, may by listening to Buddhist priests hear the right way and have begotten in them goodness, human and superhuman.

2. 護法八部 By the guardianship of 8 classes of beings such as [1] devas, [2] dragons, [3] yakchas, [4] Gandharvas, [5] Asuras, [6] Garudas, [7] Kinalos, [8] Mohowlokias (?)

Note.—(1.) *Devas* are translated heavenly beings [tien]. Although they include all in the three heavens of desire, of matter and of spirit, most of the guardians of the law are in the six Devalokas [Chap. IV.] because near in various places.

(2.) *Nagas* are translated dragons. They govern the animals.

(3.) *Yachas* are translated brave giants and also wicked tyrants. They rule demons.

(4.) *Gandharvas* are translated fragrant shades, also seekers after incense. They are joyful spirits of the gods of heaven and also rule demons.

(5.) *Asuras* are translated the not upright ones, also not the Devas, although there are four kinds still they are all of one class.

(6.) *Garudas* are translated golden-winged birds, also those who rule animals.

(7.) *Kinalos* are translated doubting gods, a new translation being singing gods. They rule demons.

(8.) *Mohowlokas* are translated those who move in their great bellies. They are the great serpent gods and also rule animals. The Chinese word chi 祇 includes the four classes of Devas, Asuras, Demons and Animals, as they have the power to reward men according to their deeds and to protect the good and control experience and thought.

3. 請法梵王 Seeking instruction from Brahma. In the six devalokas of the world of desire before one has left being independent when the desires are strong a majestic spirit is not far off. Before reaching the second meditation but after passing the self-conscious state, when virtue is esteemed but not yet attained, there is the first meditation of the great Brahma. He is the first-born in the beginning of a kalpa, therefore all devas and men call him father, consequently in all the three worlds of desire of the material and of the immaterial his authority is supreme. Although he considers himself perfect the Buddhas are not born in his mansion, yet really when all the Buddhas are perfected they must recognise Brahma as Lord. Having got the law explained sorrows can be ended.

4. 作法懺 By prayers with friends, [tso fo ts'an]. This when one has transgressed any of the 7 lighter rules and goes to a pure teacher and friends and confesses all and repents. This however can only put away the smaller sins not the great sins at the root of all.

5. 取相懺 By public litanies to all the Buddhas. For the removal of the great sin at the root of all the Shorter School [Hinayana] has no confession, but the large School [Mahayana] has. They diligently labour night and day through 5 confessions beseeching all the Buddhas and Bodhisatvas, visible and invisible, to protect and cleanse them again. But this cannot remove the 7 outrageous sins such are 1 to cause Buddhas body to bleed, 2. to kill one's father, 3. to kill one's mother, 4. to kill a Buddhist

priest, 5. to kill an atcharya, i.e. one who has finished his noviciate, 6. to destroy the Karma of a Buddhist teacher, 7. to kill the holy men of the three schools. These must in addition go through the next humiliation.

6. 無生懺 By stamping out litanies to remove the cause of sin. First in regard to all sins small or great, the ten crimes or seven outrages, there is the prayer with friends and then the public litanies, after which one must consider the sinful leak which is in one's nature so as to stop it. The penitent must sit reverently and consider solemnly that all sins are like hoar-frost or mists which the sun of wisdom when it shines can melt completely away, hence this is called the humiliation to remove the cause of sin. Or, if one has no teacher or friend with whom to have prayer, one may put up an altar and make up his mind definitely first to face the Three Precious Ones of all space and repent of one's sins and solemnly make an oath never to commit them again. Then contemplate your sins in the presence of a recluse (Aranyaka). But it is better to be determined before than after the sin is committed. By continuing in this practice then the desire to sin will be stamped out.

This uprooting of the desire pervades the four schools (Chaps. X, XI, XII, XIII) whether that cause and effect arise and disappear because there is no will of mine behind and is called uncaused; or that cause and effect are both unreal like a dream, therefore called uncaused; or that cause and effect are false and only *appear* to arise and therefore uncaused; or that cause and effect are ce pervading all sinful states, beyond expression, t fore called uncaused.

CHAPTER VII

STEPS IN THE STAGE OF *THE GROWTH* OF MORALITY. 增上戒學門

Observance of discipline produces thought; thought produces wisdom; and these are called the three infinite sciences, therefore learners of religion begin with rules, first simple and then complex, till they become complete, embracing all laws, therefore we call this growing. The Hinayana and the Mahayana schools have 7 rules each as has been already explained.

1. 在家五戒 The 5 commandments of the lay workers (Upasaka) i. e. not to kill, steal, commit adultery, lie, drink wine. Those who keep those only in part may secure the happiness of this world and that which is not of this world, but cannot be considered masters of disciples.

2. 八關齋戒 The 8 commandments of the lay-members (Upasakas). Those who keep the following for one day and one night: -- 1. not to kill, 2. not to steal, 3. not to commit adultery, 4. not to lie, 5.

not to drink wine, 6. not to soil flowers or hair or rub sessamum oil on the body, nor sing songs and dance, or lead loose lives, not to go sight-seeing and gossiping, 7. not to sit on a high big bed, 8. not to eat between meals.

If in addition to the 5 commandments the 6 fasting days of the month are also observed the gain will be greater. The six fasting days are the 8th, 14th, 15th, 23rd, 29th and 30th of each month. But when the month has only 29 days the 28th is to be kept instead of the 30th. The 1st moon, the 5th moon, and the 9th moon are called the months of constant fasting and should have 8 days of fasting and the merit will be still greater.

3. 沙彌十戒 The 10 commandments of the Sami (S'ramenara). These are monks who shave their heads, dye their clothes and follow Yu Lai, leaving their homes and become Hoshangs, i. e. Buddhist monks. Sami means to rest and to be kind-hearted, also to seek quietness. The monks must be above 7 years old and under 70. They keep 10 commandments:- 1. not to kill, 2. not to steal, 3. not to commit adultery, 4. not to lie, 5. not to drink wine, 6. not to defile incense, flowers and hair, nor rub the body with (sessamum) oil. 7. not to sing, dance or live a loose life, nor to go sight-seeing and gossiping, 8. not to sit on a high or big bed, 9. not to eat between meals, 10 not to hold possession of animals, images, or anything precious of gold or silver.

4. 持比丘律 Rules of the Bhikshus, Mendicants, Bi-Kiu. These are for those between 20 and 60 years

of age and in possession of every sense but without hindrances. They have 250 things to learn which are called the mendicant rules. The mendicants are translated as those who put off hunger, those who oppose evil, begging scholars [mendicants], the terror of devils. They are also translated as the destroyers of the enemy, desire, those who should be supported and those who do not beget any into a life of sorrow. Their 250 rules are classified into five, viz.

(1.) Those already observed which are still indispensable.

(2.) Those that are not to be learnt till about to be practised.

5. 持二部律 The second course [Bhikshu] mendicant rules. These are given to those who have kept the above rules and those of the female mendicants are considered worthy to take upon them the second course of discipline. These are divided into 5 classes but are not to be made known to those who are not ready for them, therefore we do not record them.

6. 廣持毘尼 Extensive observance of the laws [Vini] Vinaya. These are the principles of all the Buddhist Scriptures [Pitaka]. Those thoroughly versed in the literature and meaning of the Buddhist canon laws and can recite and observe them are worthy to be the guides of men and devas therefore they are many times higher. Still they have not put off the world entirely, therefore have need of public litanies.

7. 住毘尼而不動 Abiders in the law. Those who have obtained perfection in the law and are beyond any stain from breaking the law and are called those who abide immovable in the law without falling back.

8. 善能滅諍 Peacemakers. Having attained purity themselves they are able to make others pure; when disputes arise they can stop them and get all parties to yield and thus cause others to be good. In the smaller school [shing wên] this is considered the highest attainment.

9. 業清淨戒 Those who practice of purity. Boddhisatva i.e. Mahayana laymen [upasaka] and Boddhisatva monks begin in the strength of the great vow of wisdom [Puti tao, i.e. right intelligence] to preserve the seed of the spiritual nature and never to destroy it. This is the rule for the practice of fundamental purity.

10. 餘清淨戒 Superior law of purity. The Bodhisatva i.e. the apostle of the Mahayana begins in the strength of the great vow both to guard the spiritual nature and its surroundings with great care. He looks beforehand lest he breaks one of the great laws or any of the means of salvation, and he looks behind lest he falls into mean dirty ways; hence it is considered superior to the mere practice of purity.

11. 覺清淨戒 Law of conscious purity. The Bodhisatva apostles and the Bodhisatva devas leave all evil desires and evil ways and enter conscious

study of the first meditation. From this they go on to the leaving off of thought when in purity they reach the 4 meditations; when this is fixed they have no more consciousness of any sin. These are all the laws of the Mahayana school.

12. 念清淨戒 Law of pure thought. The above believe in the narrow way and realise the unseen without any thought of life and death or Nirvana. This is the law of pure thought. This is all the law of the Mahayana school.

13. 無上道戒 The unsurpassed law. This is explained by the unsurpassed wisdom which fully pervades the five commandments, the eight commandments, the ten commandments, right through to the end of all the other laws: All of these laws come from Buddha's sea of law and finally all flow back to Him again, just like different kinds of water, but have all the same wet nature; therefore such laws as the five laws, the Bhikshu laws etc. are one and all only forms, all only solemn ceremonies, all only a collection of three pure laws, as each one of them can put an end to all evil, they are called the law which includes the spirit of all law; and as each one of them can produce all sorts of good they are called the law of goodness; and as each can save all living beings they are called the law of life. Thus we include all laws as returning to wisdom, hence they are called the "returning" to the full and unsurpassed law.

CHAPTER VIII

STEPS IN THE STAGE OF GROWTH IN CONTEMPLATION. 增上定學門

If any Buddhist desires to master every virtue and obtain perfect knowledge he must get the aid of contemplation; therefore after the laws of discipline one must understand the science of contemplation. The science of contemplation embraces the three schools, Hinayana, Mahayana and the Middle school, their methods and results must be exhausted, hence we say there must be growth.

1. 六妙門禪 The six mystery gates of Nirvana [liu miao men shen] These are number, following, contemplation, reflection, returning, purity.

[1] Practise breathing [Shiu Shu]. This is to regulate harmonious breathing so as to be neither sudden nor careless ; it should be done over and over again ten times till one is perfect in it. The mind is to be included in the practice lest it wander.

[2] Practise the breath [Shiu suei]. Let the conscious mind follow conforming to the circulation of the breath through the body ten times without

exertion of strength. When the breath gets used up the state of the mind gets finer and regards frequent breathing as coarse. The mind in taking in spiritual influences should follow the breath circulating through the body and keep step with it.

[3] Practise contemplation. When the mind is gradually brought to breathe, the length of this conscious breathing in the body corresponding exactly to the breathing in and out, the mind gladly gets at rest. Then conscious following is considered coarse, and contemplation is practised to regulate the breathing of the mind, its outgoing towards all things with its return again like breath. It does not think of frequency of breath or following the breath, it has rested quietly in contemplation of all things.

[4] Practise reflection [Shiu kwan]. It is when the whole conscious being closes its eyes as it were and enters contemplation without seeing any form inward or outward but keeps the mind in contemplation, moves about in thought but is itself in one spot. This is the time for reflection.

Now this spiritual ecstasy or joy [san mei] although it returns to quietness has no wise means of salvation, it cannot put an end to the sorrows of life and death. In contemplation one sees with the eye of the mind infinitesimal thought going in and out like a breath of air, the 36 parts of the body such as skin and muscles, bones and flesh, etc. are hollow like a palm, and unclean inside, and outside most unattractive.

Again in contemplation one sees that all pleasures are in a state of decay; such decay is not a pleasure. One also sees that the mind is not incessantly reviving and dying. It does not stop for an instant and has no resting place. Again consider that good and evil are all regulated by cause and conditions, having no self-controlling nature. When one thus reflects and can, contrary to the world, see through these four courses and see no difference between man and the universe, then what has he to lean on in contemplation?

[5] Practise introspection. After practising the above four studies the reflective power is awakened and the mind goes out into the field of reflection, distinguishing between things in detail while conscious thought is going on. This is not real. So one must turn from the objects of reflection and study oneself. As reflection comes from the mind one must consider where did the mind get reflection from? etc.

[6] Practise purity [ching]. When wisdom begins to dawn in the mind then one gets back to the original pure fountain of all.

2. 十六特勝 The sixteen victories [shihliu teh shing] Avapona i.e. sent here and there. These are called victors on account of the causes and conditions being like other religions, enabling men also to cultivate the four contemplations and the four immaterial states [Chap. I. 15. Chap. V. 19-23], and are sufficient to enable men to grow into perfection hence called the 16 victories. They may be considered comparatively or progressively. We shall consider

them progressively through the realms of desire, the material and the immaterial.

[1] To know the entrance of the breath.

[2] To know the going out of the breath. It goes from the umbilicus through the nose. This corresponds with Chap. VIII. I. [1]. When the mind follows it it slowly discovers that in breathing there are two processes, the outside material air and the immaterial. It also discovers that good and evil enter with all their sorrowful consequences, that when breath stops life ceases, leaving no room for pride, for the ego is not the breath.

[3] To know the length of the breath of life this corresponds with contemplation of the world of desire and to become conscious of the impermanency of life.

[4] To know the breath pervading the whole body. This corresponds with the preparatory contemplation. When asleep though unconscious of it the breath continues. In the present state of the breath pervading the body one falls into a state of unconsciousness and enters into the state of contemplation. Gradually one feels as in a mist and something passes in and out through every pore of the skin, like breathing, and the body is felt to be unreal. One in contemplation must seek something else.

[5] To put away the body. This corresponds with the first contemplation. They find that all in the human frame is made out of the four great elements, earth, water, fire and wind, and that we come from what is outside the body.

[6] To obtain gladness. This corresponds with breaking through the gladness of the first contemplation. Once there was gladness without wise reflection, now it comes by pure contemplation and conscious reflection.

[7] To obtain pleasure. This corresponds with those breaking through the pleasure of the first contemplation. Those who have passed beyond the pleasure of elementary contemplation now learn that mere pleasure must not be one's aim.

[8] To control the mind, This corresponds with those breaking through the One Mind section of the first contemplation. The One Mind is not the human mind. When the human mind is free from sin then that is spiritual joy.

[9] To gladden the mind. This corresponds with the joy of inward purity, second contemplation. Once they could find gladness without wisdom, but now they learn that such is vain.

[10] To be able to govern oneself. This corresponds with those breaking through the One Mind section of the 2nd contemplation. Once in the second contemplation they were moved to gladness, now on the contrary they know that such is vain and so are at rest.

[11] To be delivered from self-control. This corresponds to breaking through the joy of the 3rd contemplation. Ordinary men are bound by this joy and cannot be independent of it. But now one learns that that depends on causes and conditions, therefore not real.

[12] To reflect on death. This corresponds with breaking through the unmoved joy of the 4th contemplation. Ordinary men cannot help thinking about it constantly, but now one learns that it is a state not safe from trouble.

[13] To reflect on the dissolution of matter. This corresponds with breaking through the immaterial and getting beyond the ties of matter. Ordinary men think it is emptiness and rest there, but now they learn that it is not so.

[14] To reflect on conquering all desires. This corresponds with the faculties which reach from the realm of desire right up to the immaterial. Ordinary men without the eye of wisdom think that the mind and the senses are one and are at rest. But now by wise reflection they find it is not so.

[15] To reflect on the end of all. This is to meet those of nowhereness [see Chap. V. 21]. Ordinary men think that the soul perishes but now they learn otherwise.

[16] To reflect on giving up [sacrifices?]. This is to meet those who are in the state of neither thought nor no-thought. Formerly they only sacrificed one-sidedly, now on both sides of having and not having. Ordinary people not using wise reflection call this Nirvana, but now they know what this is too.

3. 通明觀 The comprehensive reflection [Tung ming kwan].

Reflect on breath, on matter and on mind. The present state is only the result of former causes.

4. 九想觀 Nine thought reflections. [Kiu shang kwan].

[1] On swellings, [2] On bursting of swellings, [3] on bleeding, [4] on pus and sloughing of ulcers, [5] on mortification, [6] on oozings, [7] on dissolution, [8] on skeletons, [9] on cremation.

5. 八想觀 Eight belief—reflections.

[1] Buddha, [2] the law, [3] the priesthood, [4] disciplinary laws, [5] sacrifices, [6] the heavens, [7] the breath of life, [8] death.

6. 十想觀 Ten thought reflections.

[1] Of the impermanence of things, [2] of sorrow, [3] of unselfishness, [4] of purity, [5] of no joy in all the worlds, [6] of death, [7] of uncleanness, [8] of cutting off all desires to become an Arhat, [9] of caring nothing for the material or the immaterial, [10] of perfection, when the Bodhisatva desires to give a panacea to all living beings. This is the Mahayana.

7. 八背捨 Eight mortification reflections.

[1] The mortification when the man of pleasure beholds the outward form.

To do this one must have carefully observed the 5 commandments so as to be pure and must have had courage to make a great vow of glorifying the law and never give up, then let him settle down calmly and think of the big toe of the left foot, and think of it like a big bean swelling and getting black, then swelling again as large as a hen's egg. Then let him think of the second, third, fourth and fifth toes all getting like this. After that the sole of the foot, the heel, the ankle, the knee, and above it all swelling. After that let him observe the right foot swelling in the same manner. After that the parts above the waist, the loins and belly, the back and chest, and the ribs all swelling out up to the right cheek in like manner. After that let him observe carefully the neck, the crown and all the head swelling, so that the whole body is stiff from head to foot. Look at it now, only a great big swelling, most repulsive. Then look at it decaying, full of sores, blood, sweat, and pus, and worms pass through the bowels; then as the skin bursts, all the bowels full of stench protrude most repulsively. Then he will consider his body like that of a dead dog, even the beautiful bodies of beautiful men and women become so. If he still longs after the world of desire let him continue his observation of this, till there is perfect detestation of it in the heart. Desiring to leave the realms of covetousness and sensual pleasures let him with his whole mind observe again the white bones. Let him look at the temples, the skin and flesh burst open and only the white bone remaining like a great talon, everything thus bare. Above is the cracked skin and flesh on the forehead and the hair scalped off. On the crown of the head he sees the skin and flesh torn off and the skull appear. Again, from head to foot all the skin and flesh peal off, then remains the naked skeleton, joint to joint. Let him carefully consider it without motion and realize that it all arises from a definite cause. It is because of this cause that the toe bones hold the foot bones, the foot holds the ankle, knee and other bones, to the waist bones, back-bones, ribs, crown and forehead bones, teeth, and the whole skull. It is because of this cause that the crown bones are linked to the shoulder-bones, down to the arm bones, wrist-bones, palm-bones and finger-bones, all dependent on one another, the whole 360 bones. Observe them carefully, the big ones and the small ones, the strong and the weak, independent, but still there is no lord, no ego there. How the breath goes in and out of the body, but there is no body and there is no ego now. It is the same with the mind and with the law, it is all emptiness without lord or ego. Having finished this reflection one is sick of the pleasures of the body, etc. etc. Look again at the skeleton and the light of heaven shines from it. Cousider it again, at this time the soul, suddenly moves independently and begins a new life and there are eight new lights in the soul shining forth on everything. These are earth colour, water colour, fire colour, bluestone colour, yellow colour, red sunset, red colour, and snow-white colour. That is light comes to the soul like a visitor with all these, but is not of the earth. This is the fruit of the 1st meditation. [New life to the dry bones].

[2]. The mortification when the good man observes the outward form and after reflection of similar things everywhere he contemplates them with light from above, then light dawns on the heart and

great pure joy springs up from the light that is got within. This is also called the perfect 2nd contemplation.

[3]. The pure mortification. After discovering that all is unclean outside and ready to perish, it reflects still more on the state of light and gets deeper joy and delight filling the whole being. This is called the perfect 3rd contemplation and even the 4th contemplation.

[4]. Mortification in regard to space. This considers infinite space. The ordinary man thinks it immaterial but the disciples when they enter on this contemplation are never reborn again. They are beyond states and vows.

[5]. Mortification in regard to the senses.

[6]. Mortification in regard to being of no use.

[7]. Mortification in regard to the state of no-thought and of no No-thought.

[8]. Mortification in regard to ending having any thought. The disciples of Buddha hate wandering thoughts, so they enter into contemplation and stop breathing as if in nirvana [fall into a trance].

This mortification is in the Mahayana school.

8. 八勝處觀 Reflection on the eight battles.

[1]. State of worldly pleasure with little reflection whether good or bad.

[2]. State of worldly pleasure with much reflection on good and evil. One dead, a nation dying, ten thousand nations perishing, a whole continent and

even the whole world dead. One swelling and all swellings, and even all the blood and sores and sloughings in the whole world together, till one is dying of disgust. Then reflect on these cleaned of their skin and flesh, and white bones scattered all over the world. Then think of these white bones all standing up in rows and moving their hands and coming forward to you, and that you in your vision without any fear called to them and angrily said, "what do you mean by this? where do you come from?" and then you see all these falling at once on the ground again several times over. Then reflect that the light shines upon all these skeletons and they are clean!

Reflect on elephants, horses, cows and sheep, birds and beasts, then consider them as swelling corpses. Also consider meat and drink as like worms and dung; clothes, silks and cotton as like diseased skin, gold and silver like poisonous snakes, corn like dead worms, houses and gardens, country and cities, mountains and rivers, forests and jungle, all but rotten, stinking and unclean, till you see all the world a heap of uncleanness filling you with disgust. But in the vision you see, reflect how to get free from all these! hence it is called the battle with the senses [shing chi shing kien].

[3] State of no inward temptation but little reflection.

[4] State of no inward temptation but much reflection: similar to no. [2].

[5] Battling with the black.

[6] Battling with the yellow.

[7] Battling with the red.

[8] Battling with the white.

Causing the few to become many and the many to become few attaining mastery over all things, causing things to appear or disappear at will as in a dream.

The Bodhisatvas are able to show forth miraculons powers in their battles and compel the subjection of the Asuras of heaven, to surpass all other religions and deliver all living creatures. This is the Mahayana school.

9. 十一切處觀 Reflection on the ten abstract ideas.

[1] All black things. [2] All yellow things. [3] All red things. [4] All white things. [5] All lands. [6] All waters. [7] All fires. [8] All wind. [9] All space. [10] All knowledge

10. 九次第定 Contemplation of the nine steps. Beginning at the easy and going on through all the contemplations and reflections to the most difficult.

11. 師子奮迅三昧 The Master's ecstasy (sanmei). After the nine steps enter this ecstasy. It consists in putting away the desire for pleasure consciously and thoughtfully, and going through the 1st, 2nd, 3rd and 4th contemplation on to the realms of space, of knowledge, of absolutely no-place, of neither thought nor no-thought and of end of all thought. [Chap.

V. 19-23], then thorough freedom is obtained and profound peace.

12. 超越三昧 The surpassing ecstasy [chao yueh sanmei]. This follows the Master's ecstasy, and proceeds both up and down the various steps for putting away wicked desire for pleasure consciously and deliberately. If the three schools attain to this then they have mastered everything, are full of ten thousand joys, profound merit and miraculous power, meet for a perfect state.

13. 王三昧 The royal ecstasy (Wang sanmei). When one finds the true religion, all kinds of joy are found in the truth of that first act, hence called the Royal joy. Out of this come 108 or 120 or again 500 or 84,000 joys. According to others 25 joys, such as:

[1] Joy of being without spot and being saved from hell.

[2] Joy of fearing no fall and having risen through the animal kingdom.

[3] Joy of the mind at being able to rise through the state of hungry ghosts.

[4] Joy of gladness at rising above the state of asuras.

[5] Sunlight joy at escaping from the eastern continent [Chap. IV. 3].

[6] Joy like a dream at escaping from the southern continent [Chap. IV. 4].

[7] Moonlight joy at escaping from the western continent [Chap. IV. 2].

[8] Ardent joy at escaping from the northern continent [Chap. IV. 1].

[9] Unmoved joy at escaping from the 1st Devaloka [Chap. IV. 10].

[10] Uncontrollable joy at escaping from the 2nd Devaloka.

[11] Glad joy at escaping from the 3rd Devaloka.

[12] Blue joy at escaping from the 4th Devaloka.

[13] Yellow joy at escaping from the 5th Devaloka.

[14] Red joy at escaping from the 6th Devaloka.

]15] White joy at escaping from the 1st contemplation.

[16] All kinds of joy at escaping from the 3rd Brahmaloka [Chap. V. 3].

[17] Double colour joy at escaping from the 2nd contemplation.

[18] Thundering joy at escaping from the 3rd contemplation.

[19] Rain joy at escaping from the 4th contemplation.

[20] Spiritual joy at escaping from the 13th Brahmaloka [Chap. V. 13].

[21] Mirror joy at rising from the Arhat stage.

[22] Untroubled joy at rising through boundless space [Chap. V. 19].

[23] Constant joy at escaping from boundless knowledge [Chap. V. 20].

[24] Happy joy at escaping the nowhereness [Chap. V. 21].

[25] My own joy at escaping from nothought and no-nothought [Chap. V. 22].

Of the five things difficult to surpass, PARAMITA WISDOM is the very highest.

CHAPTER IX

STEPS IN THE GROWTH OF WISDOM
增上慧學門

Discipline is like seizing a thief, contemplation is like binding him, wisdom is like killing him. Having done with discipline and contemplation now it is necessary to understand Wisdom. No other religion has the wisdom to deliver one out of this world.

1. 發聲聞心 Have a mind to be a hearer of Buddha's teaching [Hinayana school] so as to know the sorrows of life, to cut off their cause, to seek quietness and end pleasure.

The sorrows of life are—the burnings and cruelties of hell, the preying of animals on one another, the plagues and starvation of hungry ghosts, the battles and wounds of the Asuras, birth, old age, sickness and death, hatreds, separation of loved ones, disappointments of all the senses amongst men; the five decaying states of the various heavens; the end of the immaterial and the returnings to go the round of transmigration again. In a word the

25 states of the 3 realms are nothing but sorrow without any true pleasure.

The way out of sorrow is by discipline to stop evil for ever; by contemplation to give up mere stray goodness, by wisdom to put an end to the false self and to put an end for ever to the trials of thought. Forced by sorrow to seek deliverance but only to save oneself without regard to other people. This is the shorter course or the Hinayana school.

2. 發辟支佛心 Have a mind to become a Pratyeka Buddha. Pratyeka means one who is self-taught [ascetic]. It is also translated enlightened by the study of a chain of causes. He reflects on the chain of 12 riddances hence called conditionally enlightened. Such a man is more intelligent than the hearers of the Hinayana school.

The 12 nidanas are these:—[1] ignorance conditions motions, [2] motions condition consciousness, [3] consciousness conditions causes, name and form, [4] name and form condition the six fields of the six senses, [5] the six fields condition contact of the senses with their objects, [6] contact conditions sensation, [7] sensation conditions desire, [8] desire conditions clinging to existence, [9] clinging to existence conditions being, [10] being conditions birth, [11] birth conditions old age, [12] old age conditions death, grief and sorrow.

When ignorance is stopped then motion stops, when motion stops the consciousness etc. stop seriatum, till grief and sorrow stop.

3. 事六度心 Have a mind to serve in the six ways of salvation. This springs up from a seed-thought of great pity in the heart. Having heard of the four truths and the twelve causes, considering himself and all living beings in the midst of the sorrows of the rounds of life and death, he thinks of some means of escape in accordance with the four truths and makes a great solemn vow.

[a] From the truth of sorrow make a vow to save all.

[b] From the truth of the causes of it make a vow to stop desire.

[c] From the truth of the way of deliverance make a vow to know it.

[d] From the truth of the extinction of sorrow make a vow to acquire perfection in it. [See also Chap. X. 2].

Having made the great vows of wisdom then proceed to practise them courageously.

[1] Show charity, giving your services, your life, and your wealth, keeping nothing back.

[2] Observe the discipline to check all sins and be as white and pure as ice and hoar-frost.

[3] Endure persecution, hating not even when beaten, cursed, flayed or cut to pieces!

[4] Progress in every good work, sparing not even one's life.

[5] Continue in contemplation, reflection and utilise the various influences till you obtain great miraculous power.

[6] Wisdom, reflecting rightly on all forces without having the 4 contrarieties (viz. in life thinking only of death, in sorrow thinking only of joy, in unselfishness only thinking of self, in vileness only thinking of purity,) though continuing through three great countless kalpas you are still untiring in your good work, such are said to have obtained the great religion that saves men. They are also called open scholars, great scholars, and superior scholars.

4. 體空觀 Body forth the reflections on the immaterial.

All things in the three worlds are but manifestations of the mind like a dreamland. This visionary character of all things should be considered. Everything that cannot be placed outside is wrongly considered to be the ego, imperfection follows and vain transmigration which all the Buddhas greatly pity. If it can be realized that all is immaterial and at the same time not cling to the emptiness of Nirvana this is the beginning of the Mahayana method. Although all things should be unreal, the remedy for the real should correspond to the unreal; if in charity you consider that there is no ego giving in charity, nor any object receiving the charity, nor any material really being given in charity, as all causes are unreal and cannot find the true reality, therefore abound in charity and never stint. This is the way in regard to the remaining five ways of salvation. (Chap. X. 3).

5. 次第三觀 Three reflections in order. In the Mahayana school it is said that all living beings have a seed of Buddha in them; that is, that their

nature is eternal and cannot be destroyed. As there are hindrances to the deliverance of this immortal part, one must—

[1] Reflect on the elements of immateriality so as to subdue the doubts which arise from experience and reason, and to ascend the steps of ten faiths [Chap XII. 1.]

[2] Must reflect on all immateriality so as to end the doubts which arise from experience and reason and to ascend the steps of the ten rests [Chap. XII. 11-20].

[3] Then reflect on entering on what is great. Stop ignorance so as to ascend the steps of the ten classes [Chap. XII. 21-30].

6. 圓頓妙觀 Reflection of the mysterious perfect mainspring called also the One Mind, from three points of view, also the great reflection and the Mahayana reflection. It is said the ONE MIND, Buddha and all living beings are really one, the result of causes and conditions. All forces have their source in immateriality. All those are Buddha's forces. Sorrow is the embodiment of them. Doubt is wisdom. Instruction is deliverance. Lose the way and you begin a round of transmigration like water getting frozen. Find the way and transmigration is at an end, thawing into water again. Although there is a vast difference between enlightenment and unenlightenment still man's true nature remains the same as Buddha's true nature. They are both one, so they have in them awakened the same

kind of great pity and great unconditioned love; they have made four great vows (Chap. IX. 3rd) to cultivate the spiritual nature in all kinds of service in the six ways of salvation (Chap. X. 3 1-6). Having saved oneself one must save others so that all may attain to the secret treasures according to his reflection and thoroughly know that which should be bodied forth is the great cause in the immaterial world which is neither weak nor tyrannical, neither united forces nor independent causes, but the unspeakable ways of spiritual virtue! It is called One Mind in three forms, most perfect and chief spring of all the supreme Mahayana. It is quiet but shines forth, it shines forth but it is quiet; hence it is called mysterious. If trials are strong reflect on six things so as to remove the cause of them.

7. 願升內院 Desire to ascend to the inner mansion of Maitreya.

In the 4th devaloka [Chap. IV. 13] there is an inner palace where the Bodhisatvas live. At present Meelé Fo [Maitreya] is preaching the law there. Those who have high aims desire to be born there and learn of him. After 80,000 human years there they come down to earth to help to preach the law. Having saved themselves they wish to save others according to their vow. In order to be born there men must practise the 10 best good deeds and practise the contemplations. [Chap. 1. 10, 12, 13.]

8. 求生淨土 Seek birth in the Pure Land.

More than ten thousand times one hundred worlds to the west is the most happy land. This is the pure Land. There at present is Omitofu [Amitabha] teaching the Law and elevating all beings. That Buddha had 48 aims [vows] to adorn the Pure Land and lead all living beings. Now he has his reward. He is in ineffable light and will live forever. His every thought is on receiving all who have opportunity to study Buddhism and be born in that country to be for ever happy without ever falling back again, and have nothing to do but hearing and believing. The most sincere in their vows then reflect on that land in order to get right, or consider Buddha's merits or his spiritual influence, or lay hold of his name, all such shall be born in that land, whether men or women, whether monk or layman, whether old or young, whether learned or foolish, whether good or bad, and even whether men or angels demons or animals, if they only believe, desire and act, they will certainly be born in that country.

All born in that country have the bodies of men or of devas, and all are of golden hue growing out of the lotus, beautiful and perfect without ever having again to suffer from the troubles of life. They all ascend to the place prepared for them.

Therefore all the classics and essays praise Him with all their might and the Wha Yen king, in the chapter Hing Yuen Pin, says, "I desire when I die to put off everything that clouds and hinders my seeing that God face to face and then I shall be born in his happy temple above." The hymn of the Mahayana school at the beginning of the Leng Kia King says,

All monks of all lands, Pusas 'mid all men,
Buddhas of all kinds, carnate and reforming,
Come from Paradise, from the Everlasting.

In southern India the illustrious Bikshu Nagardjuna [about A. D. 194] was able to break through the school of the soul being neither existing nor non-existing and got to the first land of joy, and ascended into the happy country. And the books, the *Pao Chih, Pan Yo, Leng Yen, Fa Hwa, Ki Shin Lun*, etc. 寶積 般若 楞嚴 法華 起信論 all of them direct the way to this happy land. And the books, *Ta Chih Hien Hu King, Ku Yin Wang king, Shihliu Kwan king, Wu Liang Shiu king, Omito king, Wang Seng lun*, etc. 大集賢護經 鼓音王經 十六觀經 無量壽經 阿彌陀經 往生論 are special guides without any other object.

Again only here do the common people and the sages live together in the Pure Land, so they are able to be prepared to ascend crosswise to the three Pure lands. Therefore even common men attending to their business have also their share here and all the great Pusas also live in the same land.

CHAPTER X

THE STEPS IN THE ORTHODOX (OR ECLECTIC) SCHOOL. 藏教位次門

Both the Hinayana and the Mahayana schools have the three distinctions into Sacred books, Laws and Discussions [Tripitaka] but these are not the same in the two schools. So we now only refer to that which is true in the three, hence called the Orthodox school.

We do not call it the Hinayana as it includes also the 12 nidanas serving in the six paths etc. (Chap. IX. 2, 3) all of which belong to the three schools equally. Its Sacred books are Sz Ahan etc. explaining the three studies of Discipline, Contemplation and Wisdom. Its Laws (Vinaya) are Sz Fen, Wu Fen, Ken Pen, Tseng Ki, Shi Sung, Shen Kien, Kiei Yin Yeien, Vi Ni Mu, etc. explaining how to grow in the Law and in Contemplation. Its Discussions (Ahidharma) such as Ta Pi Po Sha, Ku Shie Lun, etc. also explain growth in Contemplation and growth in Wisdom. So this Orthodox school has steps belonging to the three schools, eleven of the Hinayana school, only one of the Middle school and four of the Mahayana. Although different in some respects they are one in the practice of the five reflections (Chap. X. 5), one in putting an end to the senses and reason, one in getting out of the realms of desire, of matter and of the immaterial, and one in proving their truth, so that the willow leaves (i. e. men) may cease from weeping and be at rest.

1. 五停心 Five heart rests.

(1) Let unsatiable men reflect on uncleanness as in the nine thoughts, eight mortifications etc. (Chap. VIII 4-7).

(2) Let angry men reflect on kindness and tenderheartedness as in the four boundless hearts, etc. (Chap. II. 14).

(3) Let the mad and foolish reflect on causes (Chap. I. IX. 2), so as to get at the fruit without a cause, i. e. first cause (Chap. X. 5].

[4] Let the selfish world reflect on the elements of the world [Chap. X. 5], earth, water, fire and wind, out of which the immaterial mind and the six senses are made without any ego. Let the beclouded world reflect on Buddha, the ten graces of Buddha so as to put off sin; such as the reflection on the eight thoughts [Chap. IV. 5], reflection on Buddha.

[5] Let the lost scattered world reflect on breathing and the six mysterious gates [Chap. VIII.

1]. In one word the five heart-rests consist in one method, viz. stop sin in the heart then you will have rest.

2. 別相念 Think of another state.

[1] First reflect that the body is unclean.

[2] Reflect how we suffer pain.

[3] Reflect how the mind is not permanent.

[4] Reflect that the Law is impersonal.

All men in regard to the five conditions of being crosswise (i. e. making a short cut to Paradise without going through the rounds of transmigration) rejoice constantly in their purity and the four paradoxes [Chap. X. 3], hence it is necessary to reflect on the 36 impurities of the body etc. The human mind exists only for a moment; good and evil are permanent but without a governor neither is independent. In this way put an end to the four paradoxes and become truly perfect.

3. 總相念 Think of the general state.

Reflect that as the body is impure then the sensations of the mind are impure also.

As the sensations are painful then the ways of the body and mind are also painful.

Reflect that as the mind perishes the movements of the body perish.

Reflect that as the law is unselfish or universal then the mind in the body should be also universal and unselfish.

Have four reflections for the four states to put an end to the four paradoxes so as to become perfect.

4. 煖位 The hot zeal stage.

After reflecting well on the four thoughts advance with courage to put off evil and produce goodness. Check uncommitted evil and put an end to what has been committed. Advance unwrought good and increase what has been commenced. Depart from the sin of desultory diligence and let the state of the four truths produce something like deliverance in you. As in producing fire, by boring wood before the fire burns, heat is first felt; so we call this the hot stage.

5. 頂位 The mountain-top stage.

Practise well the four feet of your heart's desire so that you may climb high and see all things as clearly as the four points of the compass from the mountain-top. The four feet of the heart's desire are

[1] The foot of glad longing for the subjects of contemplation.

[2] The foot of incessant thinking of them.

[3] The foot of progress in their study.

[4] The foot of wise contemplation. This last is also called the reflecting foot and the thoughtful foot.

Know that these are the means used for the accomplishment of the eight contemplations. This contemplation is called the contemplation of the heart's desire as one gets all he wishes and is able to exhibit all kinds of divine power [miracles]. One cannot stay long in this stage. If one does not advance he falls behind and this is called falling from the top!

6. 忍位 The stage of perseverance.

Out of these four feet grow five kinds of goodness which become rooted in the four truths and persevere and delight in them without ever falling back, hence called the persevering stage.

[1] The first is the believing root, belief in the four truths which produce the perfect root of contemplation, deliverance and peace.

[2] The second is a progressive root—with plans for progress.

[3] The third is a thinking root—how to get hold of helpful truths and not allow any evil to enter.

[4] The fourth is a contemplating root—keeping the heart in the right way.

[5] The fifth is the wisdom root—controlling contemplation.

7. 世第一位 The highest stage in the world. This is an advanced stage when by the power of faith, the power of progress, the power of thought, the power of contemplation and the power of wisdom [see No. 6] one gets truly perfect and unsurpassed on earth.

8. 初果須陀洹 The **first degree of graduation** n Buddhist saintship [Scrotapana].

After gaining perfection through the above five powers, the eight perseverances, and eight learnings, one gets to see immaterial truth—the branch of seven enlightenments. The first is Scropatana, meaning a graduate and junior, also opposer of the customs of the world. The eight learnings and those four truth reflections etc. which one needs in order to get through all the [eight] sorrows of life. The branch of seven enlightenments are [a] thought enlightenment, [b] law enlightenment, [c] enlightenment in progress, [d] enlightenment in joy, [e] enlightenment about things to be put away, [f] enlightenment about contemplation, [g] enlightenment about mortification.

When these are mastered one peacefully enters on the "Eight paths" which are:—

[1] Right faith, [2] Right resolve, [3] Right speech, [4] Right action, [5] Right progress, [6] Right contemplation, [7] Right thought, [8] Right destiny. This is the perfect and holy way.

Those who depend on Julai's power do not fall into annihilation.

9. 二果斯陀舍 The **second degree of graduation** in Buddhist saintship [Sakridagamin]. A planter of thought and truth who has put an end to half the trials of life and who as soon as born can put an end to doubt, he is also called an enlightened one.

10. 三果阿那舍 The **third degree of graduation** in Buddhist saintship [Anagamin]. He has put an entire end to the trials of the world of desire and

will never be born again in the realm of desire but only in the real immaterial worlds and there he puts an end to doubts.

11. 四果阿羅漢 The **fourth degree of graduation** in Buddhist saintship [Arhat]. He has put an entire end to the trials of the three worlds [of desire of the material and of the immaterial world] called also "the destroyer of the thief" i.e. "conqueror of all passions", one who is "deserving of worship" exempt from rebirth, one who has reached the truth.

[Note. The above eleven steps are those of the Hinayana school.]

12. 中乘辟支佛果 The **degree of Pratyeka** Buddha of the Middle school.

This one after hearing the twelve chain of causes [Chap. IX. 2] has his hair on end and his tears flow. Then he does much good, worships the Buddhas much, and hears much of the law. The quickest attain the Pratyeka degree in four generations while the slowest take one hundred.

[*Note.*—This is the only degree of the middle school.]

13. 大乘初阿僧祇滿 The **first degree of the Mahayana school.** These are the Pusas who from the time they made their four great vows have extensively served in the six ways of salvation [Chap. IX. 3] and have saved and benefitted others, and have abounded in every goodness and wisdom, who have sought light and

honoured all Buddhas, who have kept themselves always clear of women and the four evil states of existence [Chap. III.] and have diligently and courageously passed through innumerable trouble, not thinking of pain, are called the 1st degree of in the stage of four thoughts not having reached the hot zeal stage, [Chap. X. 4.]

14. 二阿僧祇滿 The **second degree of the Mahayana.**

They are those of the first degree who have untiringly continued in a similar course through innumerable kalpas and who have been recorded in the presence of all the Buddhas. These are in the hot zeal stage.

15. 三阿僧祇滿 The **third degree of the Mahayana.**

They are those of the second degree who have again made a great vow to come down to earth to reform men and who have abounded still more in goodness and wisdom and passed through endless kalpas or troubles so that they might be perfect.

16. 藏教佛果 **Buddhaship** of the Orthodox school.

After completing the third degree they appear in the fourth devaloka [Chap. IV. 13] for rebirth and they give themselves to religion and sit cross-legged under the tree of wisdom when suddenly springs forth the 34 perfect aims and suddenly all evil is cut off and all truth is practised in perfection till one gets all knowledge; such as the three lights [Heaven's eye, the origin of life, the dawn of life]; the six penetrations [Heaven's eye, Heaven's ear, earth's heart, the realm of the gods, origin of life, dawn of life?]; the ten powers, [1 conscience, 2 knowledge, 3 joy, 4 root of knowledge, 5 desire of knowledge, 6 the nature of knowledge, 7 supreme truth, 8 the origin of life, 9 Heaven's eye, 10 the dawn of life?]; the four fearlessnesses; the 18 superior ways of Buddha [for description of each see Buddhist Numerical Dictionary]. The 32 notes of Buddha; the 80 signs of Buddha; the 3 preachings of the Law for the salvation of all. All such are called the fruits of Buddhaship in the Orthodox or Eclectic school.

This is the highest degree of this school. It is full of compassion to save all beings and may reside in various mansions with freedom to act according to circumstances. Those who have attained this are a body with power to act suddenly and meet any emergency. They are Buddhas.

If such again voluntarily descend to the stage of Bodhisatvas they break through the ordinary four truths and have no means of showing that the three persons are only One Being. These four stages belong to the Mahayana school.

CHAPTER XI

THE STEPS OF THE BROAD SCHOOL.

通教位次門

The Broad or Union school gets that name as it is connected with the schools before and after it. It has no special books of its own except those of the Mahayana school, said to belong to all the three schools alike. The following belong to this school.

1. 乾慧地 The attainment of heavenly wisdom. Here one sees the way the body is controlled by the mind as if it were only a dream. Although one has not attained to a state of zeal when one can control things as water, still wisdom has taken a profound effect, hence it is called Heavenly wisdom.

2. 性地 The attainment of the spiritual nature. This is when one reflects on how to stop the round of life and death and has produced hot zeal [Chap. X. 4] to plant the four kinds of goodness and to reach a state like perfection.

3. 八人地 The eight human patiences. In religion there are 16 states of the mind, viz. the eight instructions for the eight endurances. In incessant joy patience is fuller than instruction, hence called eight patiences.

4. 見地 The attainment of sight. The eight instructions are complete and one can see the true principle of the real unseen and cut off the evil ways of the senses and doubt.

5. 薄地 The attainment of leanness as to the world. Thus when half the wrong thoughts of the world of desire are cut off and the trials get gradually less thick, hence it is called the thin attainment.

6. 離欲地 The attainment of freedom of desire. This is when the thoughts and doubts of the world of desire are all gone.

7. 已辦地 The attainment of finished work. This is when all the doubts of the three realms are completely gone and they have become Arhats, hence called finished or completed ones [Chap. X. 11] Here the traditional school i.e. the Hinayana remains. But the Pusas do not remain at this attainment but pass on higher.

8. 辟支佛地 The attainment of the state of Pratyeka Buddha [see Chap. X. 12]. This is the highest attainment of the middle school [Madhyimayana].

9. 菩薩地 The attainment of Pusaship [see Chap. IV. 14]. The pusas, besides attaining to all that the two lower schools have attained to, further diligently strive to benefit and save others and have miraculous powers to cleanse the world. This stage surpasses for ever the glory of the other two schools.

10. 佛地 The attainment of Buddhaship. When the Budhisatvas have made a vow to benefit all living beings and when their work is perfected so that

their thoughts correspond to the true wisdom all evil is cut off and they attain the very highest wisdom, full of all the powers of the Buddhas whether manifested under the tree of wisdom—a glorious state like the king of the Sumeru mountain, seated on the great ocean or manifested in the highest mountains of the visible world [see Chap. V. 18], with bodies gigantic in size and able to assume millions of forms, to fill the universe with them, but all holy in character. These are not called Pusa of the Union school. They attain these mysterious results in the unseen world. In other respects they are the same as those of the Orthodox school.

CHAPTER XII

THE STEPS OF THE NEW SCHOOL [MAHAYANA]. 別教位次門

Those going in for this must first believe in the nature of Buddha according to the Middle school [10th stage]. After that they cultivate the three meditations or Reflections [Chap. IX. 5] each in its order. This is the way of the Mahayana Bodhisatvas alone. It is different from the Hinayana and Madhyimayana Pi tsz Fo in its doctrines, its principles, its wisdom, its putting off of evil, its practice, its grades, its causes, its effects, all are different from the former—the Primary and the Middle schools, and also different from the complete school below, therefore we call it the different or the new school. The difference of doctrine is about Bodhisatvas, the difference of principles is following the three truths; the difference about wisdom is the order of the three wisdoms; the difference in steps is in the order of the three doubts; of practice, the five kinds do not match; of cause, if one cause fails then one result fails.

From the practice of the three reflections in their order, therefore externally there are 10 beliefs, internally three classes of worthies of 10 attributes and 10 different stages of saintship, and afterwards there are of eternal and mysterious knowledge, making altogether 52 different subjects beginning with the simple and ending with the more profound, all with their respective results independent of one another.

1. 十心 **The ten aims** [also called Ten Faiths [Chap. XIII. 2].

[1] 信心 To have Faith. I have heard that the cause of all suffering lays hold of the four infinite truths [Chap. IX. 3] together with Buddha's nature of the Middle school and constantly dwells on the principles of the three Precious Ones and follows them unswervingly. This is Faith.

[2] 念心 To have thoughtfulness. After believing in Buddha's nature [of love] and thinking of it incessantly then there springs up wisdom in the heart which puts on the armour of a great vow. This is thoughtfulness.

[3] 精進心 To progress. Having made a great vow one then diligently cultivates cessation from all evil and reflection. This is progress.

[4] 慧心 To have wisdom. After reflection put an end to doubt. This is wisdom.

[5] 定心 To have contemplation. After progress and wisdom there is formed a character.

[6] 不退心 To have perseverance. This is by going through 37 lessons to subdue trials.

[7] 護法心 To defend the doctrine.

[8] 迴向心 To return to the Source. Some peace is attained and no more growth in conceit.

[9] 戒心 To have self-control. Not yielding to the devils of overstrength or over-weakness but quietly and firmly keeping from evil.

[10] 願心 To have a desire to save others. Not to love imperfection but to have pity on those who are imperfect and a desire to save them.

11–20. 十住 **The Ten Grades.**

[11] 初發心住 The growing grade. When the Pusas have kept their Faith and have attained perfection in spite of many trials and have put an end to personal considerations from which so many sorrow arise and can see the principles of true spirituality, pitying that men are deluded and constantly contriving how to save them; this is called the growing grade.

It ranks with the degree of Su-to-yuen [Chap. V. 8, XII. 2].

[12] 治地住 The grade of submitting to rule. It constantly follows the mind of the spiritual world and purifies all the ways of life.

This grade ranks with preparation for Sz-to-han [Chap. X. 9].

[13] 修行住 The grade of cultivating goodness. It cultivates every good.

This ranks with Sz-to-han attained.

[14] 生貴住 The grade of noble birth. This is when one is born into Buddha's family and gets a holy heart.

This ranks with preparation for Anahau [Chap. X. 10].

[15] 方便具足住 The grade of perfect means. This is when one studies the roots of infinite goodness. This ranks with Anahan attainment [Chap. X. 10].

[16] 正心住 The grade of right mind. This is when one has mastered wisdom. This ranks with preparation for A-lo-han (Arhat) [Chap. X. 11].

[17] 不退住 The no retrogression grade. This is when one has reached the unseen world from which there is no falling back to rebirth. This ranks with the attainment of A-lo-han.

[18] 童眞住 Grade of immortal youth. This is when no evil can lead one astray from wisdom and is free from all sin. Ranks with Pratyeka Buddha [Chap. X. 12].

[19] 法王子住 Grade of heirs of the King of Law. Buddha is King of Law. Those born of Princes of this Law are the children of the King of Truth. This ranks with the Pusas of the Broad School.

[20] 灌頂住 The Ordained grade. Being Buddha's successors they must have Buddha's knowledge. Having put off all the doubts of the world and understood the ordinary truths they are worthy to be ordained as Teachers of men and devas.

21 - 30 十行 The Ten Characteristics.

Those who have passed through the unseen to the Cause and who have learned how to be saved from this world and practise all the good powers of Buddha which we call the ten attributes, have 10 characteristics.

[21] 歡喜行 The characteristic of joy. This is added to the 1st Paramita of alms so as to create joy in others.

[22] 饒益行 The characteristic of forgiveness, This is added to the 2nd Paramita of morality so as to include a desire to save others.

[23] 無瞋恨行 The characteristic of no hatred or anger. This is added to the 3rd Paramita of patience so as not to be spiteful but humble and respectful.

[24] 無盡行 The characteristic of being irresistible. This is added to the 4th Paramita of energy so as to break down all opposition.

[25] 離痴亂行 The characteristic of being free from fanaticism. This is added to the 5th Paramita of Contemplation. As there is wisdom, there is no madness.

[26] 善現行 The characteristic or power of manifestation. This is added to the 6th Paramita of wisdom.. These are always born in the presence of the Buddhas and understand all laws.

[27] 無著行 The characteristic of having no will of one's own. This is added to the 7th Paramita of means, so that in regard to life and death or Nirvana there is no self-will.

[28] 尊重行 The characteristic of honour. This is added to the 8th Paramita of vows as the root of all good, most honourable and most difficult.

[29] 善法行 The characteristic of organizing. This is added to the 9th Paramita of enterprise, so that things may be accomplished according to plans.

[30] 眞實行 The characteristic of truth. This is added to the 10th Paramita of knowledge so as to know the true nature of things.

31-40 十廻向 **The Ten returns.**

The ten grades lead to the Real Unseen, the ten characteristics lead to see the difference between the true and the false.

To return from these two extremes in order to attain religion is what is meant by the ten returns.

[31] 救護衆生離衆生相廻向 Return to save all by leaving their present state. Not to remain in empty immaterialism but to save men; not to let men live in false appearances but to deliver them from their present state. This double action of right reflection enables one to be in the six paths of existence without their suffering. But ordinary and non-Buddhists those of the two schools cannot comprehend this.

[32] 不壞廻向 Return to the indestructible. The immaterial has two limits [Chap. XII. 4] both of which may perish but between them there is what is indestructible.

[33] 等一切佛廻向 Return to equality with all the Buddhas. In this state all the works of the Buddhas throughout the three realms can be practised.

[34] 至一切處迴向 Return to omnipresence. By the power of the great vow one reaches all kingdoms in the universe and worships all the Buddhas.

[35] 無盡功德藏迴向 Return to inexhaustible treasures. Always living at the fountain of the law of existence one confers its blessings on all seekers.

[36] 隨順平等善根迴向 Return to the obedience of Eternal goodness. This is to bring back all men to practise every good and carry out Buddha's ways without any other desire.

[37] 隨順等觀一切衆生迴向 Return of all beings to the obedience of Eternal reflection. All good and evil are phases of one true state.

[38] 眞如相迴向 Return to the Archytype, the **True Form.** This is when the heart obtains freedom like the Buddhas of the three realms.

[39] 無縛解脫迴向 Return to deliverance from bondage. This reflects all the forces of the three realms. Though immaterial they are not nonentities but unchained powers.

[40] 法界無量迴向 Return to the infinite spiritual realm. This is when one gets enlightened in regard to all cosmic laws.

41-50. **The ten attainments.**

What delivers all sentient beings from the round of existence is called attainment.

[41] 歡喜地 Attainment of gladness. This is got first by getting rid of ignorance and then finding truth, giving up independent natures and uniting

them; hence there is great joy and gladness. This is the beginning of pure and perfect reward when one can appear in various forms in the hundred worlds of Buddhas for the benefit of all. Here one finds out that this religion is complete. It is only vaguely found in the different religions.

[42] 離垢地 Attainment of holiness. This is when one has found pure truth, leads a holy life, far removed from any of the petty sins that bring sorrow.

[43] 發光地 Attainment of power to give light. This is when one has completed the highest contemplation and is able to shed infinite mysterious light on men.

[44] 燄慧地 Attainment of burning wisdom. This is when one dwells calmly in the highest wisdom and all sorrows are burnt up like fuel.

[45] 難勝地 The attainment which is difficult to surpass. This is when the knowledge of truth and the customs of the world are not made to clash with one another, but one yields to the other easily.

[46] 現前地 The attainment of power as if ever-present. This is when one knows the results from the causes as if actually present, and to lead the Eternal and most supreme wisdom to act as if present before one.

[47] 遠行地 The far-distant attainment. This is when one has reached the immaterial grade with its after service beyond this world and beyond mere deliverance from the world.

[48] 不動地 The attainment of the undisturbed state. This is when with undivided wisdom one can proceed undisturbed by trials.

[49] 善慧地 The attainment of holy wisdom. This is when one has mastered the mystery of life, The four all-pervading things, and is able to make this law known everywhere.

[50] 法雲地 The attainment of wisdom's fountain. This is when all virtue is gathered in great laws as water is in the clouds from which come showers full of blessing on all.

[51] 等覺菩薩 The **attainment of Pusaship** of universal enlightenment.

When wisdom fills every place and one enters into the presence of the Holy of Holies beholding it as in cloud and darkness—clouds of Heaven in the religious world,—this is called **Buddhahood**; if looking to the understanding of mysteries it is also called Pusaship, therefore we call it **Eternal enlightenment** beyond which there is no advance.

[52.] 別教妙覺佛位 The attainment of the mysterious enlightenment of Buddhaship according to the Mahayana school. On the Pure Soul finally dawns a great awakening by which one spiritually understands the origin of things, ignorance is completely removed and light quietly shines.

Those revealing the Archetype, True Form, are called the "law body", [Chap. XIII. 3].

Those harmonising the four wisdoms with pure knowledge and the sacred presence into "becoming" are called the self producing "rewarding bodies."

Those whom we on earth call Pusas and place on Lotus pedestals in glorious temples of great glory, are called "bodies of empassing transformations."

These appearing in the highest material heavens and having the tallest bodies are called Tai Lie transformation bodies and great transformation bodies.

Those less intelligent among the Fusas or learned among ordinary men who can under the tree of wisdom manifest their bodies as men, these by their parents are called poor transformation bodies, also the million transformations.

Those appearing in all sorts of forms are called transformation bodies according to circumstances.

In all these ignorance has not been fully removed and they have not reached the perfect and unsurpassed wisdom, they are not called the highest attainment of mysterious enlightenment. Only the intelligent of the Mahayana school say that ignorance is all gone and perfect enlightenment attained. But this mysterious enlightenment is the Perfect Mysterious Enlightenment.

CHAPTER XIII

THE STEPS OF THE COMPLETE SCHOOL

圓教位次門

Having perfect mystery, perfect fulness, perfect sufficiency and perfect efficiency this school is called the Perfect School. All the results brought about by the causes and conditions of life come from the great Cause in the immaterial world. It is the three truths [of One Mind, the immaterial and the material] working perfectly and incomprehensively. This is the **perfect mystery.** From three thousand principles there are created three thousand things. From observing three thousand things we infer three thousand principles. Things and their principles are perfectly seen. When we think of sufficiency it is perfect sufficiency. If you do not understand it, it is not less; if you understand it, it is not more. When things are already perfect and their substance is not gradually getting to be perfect this is perfect efficiency. Hence we say the three states One Mind, Buddhas and all beings are one without any difference. All beings are the

Archetype, Buddhas are the Archetype, the One Mind is the Archetype. There are no two Archetypes. One kind of incense for each kind of form is only the Middle school. All ways are nothing but Buddha's ways. The three schools above and all living beings have never gone beyond this principle. But we are ignorant because in daily use, although in daily use we are unconscious of it. If we only once become conscious of it then it would be like practising "not being" mad going straight ahead. After the disease is cured then the show of the world is all vanity. Therefore it is said the full and perfect wisdom returns to where it cannot add anything. But the perfection explains everything and everything is perfect. Wise words to govern the world benefit production without hindering one another. Moreover the three schools above have gained power because of the truth in them, and is it not because each of them has perfect mystery?

The attainments of Buddhaships in the above schools were not really so, only generally speaking they were. As compared with the Perfect School they are only preparatory.

1. 圓五品位 The place of **five arts.**

(1 The art of being happy, following the mysterious law. Having attained happiness oneself makes others happy.

(2) The art of studying to strengthen one's principle, is finished and a solemn vow influences the mind to benefit one's neighbours.

[2] The art of studying to strengthen one's principles. It is like adding fat to the fire and gives greater light.

[3] The art of preaching when reflection on principles is finished and a solemn vow influences the mind to benefit one's neighbours.

[4] The art of partly practising the six ways of salvation [Chap. IX. 3] when reflections on principles are thoroughly ripe and action is taken so as to be able to do some small service in charity and in the immaterial and universal powers, [Chap. I 14] and likewise in discipline.

[5] The art of fully practising the six ways of salvation. By one's own example causing others to do the same—complete in word and deed, thoughtful and consecrated, surpassing anything gone before.

2. 圓十信位 The place of the **ten Faiths**—all of which are Buddhalike in character.

[1] Faith in good exercise of the universals [Chap. I. 14].

[2] Faith in good exercise of the vow of pity and in having thoughtfulness.

[3] Faith in good exercise of the reflection on the Perfect Mystery and in having a progressive mind.

[4] Faith in thoroughly ending the three doubts and in having wisdom.

[5] Faith in thoroughly knowing the whole universe and in having contemplation.

[6] Faith in cultivating well the arts of the Perfect Mystery [Chap. XIII. 1] and in getting beyond fear of falling back.

[7] Faith in helping well in religion and in having a mind to defend religion.

[8] Faith in knowing well the steps of progress and in having a mind to return [Chap. XII. 4].

[9] Faith in practising well calm endurance and having the mind under discipline.

[10] Faith in cultivating well having no reserves [likings] and in having a willing heart.

These although they have the same name as the ten aims of the Mahayana school are very different. The Mahayana school uses the reflection on life and death and by the study of Cause enters the immaterial and is thereby just able to control the troubles of sight and thought. But the Perfect school uses the three reflections of the Mystery even to the reflection of the nature of Law itself and perfectly subdues ignorance.

These ten Faiths are also divided into Elementary, Intermediate and Advanced.

3. 圓十住位 The place of the **ten Grades** each of which should attain to Buddhahood. It is also called the state of waking up to Buddhahood. The Mahayana school uses the reflection of how not to cause sorrow, the elementary grade, etc., but is only able to put an end to the trouble in this world alone. By the use of the reflection of the One Mind in three forms [Chap. IX. 6, XIII. opening] one may end

ignorance and be able to be a Buddha in a hundred worlds ranking with the attainment of gladness in the new school [Chap. XII. 5]. It is right enlightenment attaining the wisdom-body without outside help. It is the pure mysterious Law-body, brightly supplying everything.

The Wisdom-Body is the character or attribute of Wisdom, which understands clearly the causes of things, and wisdom grows.

The Body of Mysterious Law is the character or attribute of the mysterious Body which rights causes, and grows principles.

The responding Body is the character or attribute of Salvation which conditions causes, and grows goodness. [Chap. X. 7]. This ranks with the attainment of Wisdom's fountain of the Mahayana school [Chap. XIII. 5 [10].

This is like the moon. Although its real body does neither grow more nor less still as the dark part grows less the bright part sheds more light.

4. 四十行位 The place of the **ten characteristics.**

After passing the steps of the ten grades and ting an end to the ten kinds of ignorance then me the characteristics which have the same name as those of the New School only that the first characteristics of joy in this school ranks with the universal enlightenment of the Pusas of the New Buddhism school [Chap. XII. 6]. The Forgiveness of this school ranks with that of the Mysterious Enlightenment of the Buddhas [Chap. XII. 7]. Still the perfect full recompensated Buddha of the Mahayana school is not that of the second characteristic of the Perfect School but much the same as the mysterious enlightenment of the Buddhas in the Perfect School.

5. 圓十廻向位 The place of the **ten returns.** The names are the same as those of the Mahayana school, but it is after passing the characteristics and breaking through the ten ignorances that one reaches the ten returns.

6. 圓十地位 The place of the **ten attainments.**

After the ten returns and breaking through another kind of ignorance then one reaches the ten attainments. Though the names are the same as those of the New School they are totally different.

7. 圓等覺位 The place of **universal enlightenment.** After the ten Attainments and putting off another kind of ignorance one enters the place of universal enlightenment, the sea of change into life and death with only one birth more to go through, therefore called the One birth-bound Pusa.

8. 金剛後心 The place of the Pure Diamond. After the universal enlightenment comes the Pure Diamond. When the wisdom of Heaven reaches the Universal enlightenment one reaches the first grade of Heaven's wisdom and after going through it twelve times then he reaches the full Mysterious Enlightenment and obtains the unsurpassed Religion.

CHAPTER XIV

THE PURE LAND CROSS-PASSAGE SHORT CUT SCHOOL

淨土橫超門

There are four lands of the Buddhas, viz.

[1] The land where the ordinary men and saints live together. If the coarse elements prevail then they are in the midst of sorrow, hence it is called the mixed world such as the Saha world ["the inhabited portion of every universe" Eitel]. But if the better elements prevail then they are the good companions of men and devas, hence it is called the Pure Land such as the Western Paradise.

[2] The land where there is abundant goodness. If gone there from analysing immateriality [Chap. X. 5 [1]] then will be sunk in calm leakings of immaterialism; hence it is called imperfectly clean. But if skilfully delivered by bodying forth the immaterial [Chap. IX. 4] then you may see Buddha and hear the Law; hence it is called Pure.

[3] The Land where there is the glory of real recompense. If reached through the three reflections

in order [Chap. IX. 5] although equally perfect with those who have experienced religion still ignorance is great and wisdom is rather imperfect; hence it is called imperfectly clean. If reached from the reflections of the One Mind [Chap. IX. 6] although it is not different from the Law-world still there is some slight ignorance left, but Wisdom is intelligent, hence it is called Pure.

[4] The land of calm light. If we speak generally the New school only cuts off 12 different kinds of ignor-anees and has not fully reached the fountain of Law; hence it is called imperfectly clean. If we speak generally of the Perfect School it has cut off all the 42 kinds of ignorances and has reached the essence of spiritual nature; hence it is called Pure.

But these four lands of the Buddhas are again reached in two different ways, namely, lengthwise and crosswise. If in all steps from beginning to end one depends on one's own strength this is called reaching the Pure Land lengthwise i.e. by the long route of transmigration. But if in all efforts one depends on the grace or prayer of Amitabha, although one has not been able to cut oneself free from experience he is yet able to leave the evil [Saha] world and get to the pure land of Paradise. Once there he can get to the Pure Lands of goodness, real recompense, and calm light, without sacrificing himself to save himself and afterward attain entrance. This is called reaching the Pure land cross-wise or by a short cut.

Speaking generally of the difference of the four schools:—

The Hinayana School analyses the immaterial. It attains its end by analysis of the immaterial [Chap. IX. 5 [1]. It leaves surrounding imperfect purity, employs imperfect means, but cannot attain to a life of perfect purity, how much less reach the Pure Land of goodness.

The Broad School attains its end by thoughtfully embodying the immaterial. It leaves surrounding imperfect purity, employs pure means and lives in purity before cutting off doubt.

The New School knows that elsewhere there is a kingdom of Buddha. If while in the stage of the ten Faiths [Chap. XII. 1] one makes a vow to go there then he shall reach the Pure Land. If he does not make that vow he cannot get there; the cultivation of the various grades, characteristics and returns [Chap. XII.] enable him to get to the pure land of goodness. The attainment to universal enlightenment of Pusas only enables one to attain the imperfectly clean state of real recompense. The attainment of the Mysterious enlightenment of Buddha only enables one to experience the imperfectly clean calm light.

The Perfect School. If in the stage of Five Arts [Chap. XIII. 1] one can make a vow he will get to the three intermediate positions in the Pure Land [Chap. XVI. 5–7]. If he does not make the vow then the is not sure to get there. If in the stage of Ten Faiths of the Perfect School one makes a vow, he will get to the three advanced positions in the Pure Land, i. e. he by a short cut enters the Pure Land of goodness.

Having found out how to stop the cause of sorrow then he by a short cut reaches the Pure Land of real recompense and of calm light. If one does not make a vow then he must go on through seven Faiths before he reaches the Pure Land of goodness.

But those who have attained to the 1st grade [Chap. XIII. 3] and upwards, whether they have made a vow or not, shall reach the Pure Land of real recompense and the Pure Land of Calm Light. Therefore so far as they depend on themselves in the cultivation of religion all the four schools may be termed those who are being saved by the long route. Only that which depends on the power of the grace or prayer of Amitabha is saved by the short cut.

The objector asks:—When all sorts of evil attack men's hearts, and men and devas have little good, if a man prays, repents, [Chap. VI. 4-6] returns and vows he can go to the Western Paradise, how is it that the Orthodox and Broad schools cannot get there? We answer, those of these two schools have never so much as heard the name of the Buddha of this new country. If they hear of the ten thousand virtues of this Amitabha and desire to be born in that land, then they shall have found the secret of power of the New and the Perfect Schools.

1 淨土疑城 The Doubting city of the Pure Land.

The Council of the Everlasting Ju Lai says that Buddha spoke to Mee le saying, If any one who has fallen into doubt repents and abounds in all goodness, Buddha's knowledge, universal knowledge, infinite knowledge, incomparable knowledge, knowledge of supreme holiness, all-embracing knowledge, and cannot believe it possible by depending entirely on himself, but having heard the name of Buddha believes it possible; although born in the Pure Land they cannot appear with the Lotus Buddhas [i. e. those delivered from the filth of this world as the Lotus opens into flower out of the mud] for 500 years they cannot see Buddha nor hear the Law, nor see the Pusas and the followers of the Hinayana School, and cannot worship nor serve the Buddhas and cannot enquire about the treasures of Pusaship. If he can depart from all kinds of things which destroy high virtue and all the sins of the past then he may come out among them. You should know that to doubt is to do a great injury.

Thus we see that it is belief in another and not in self. Before opening up the way to the perfect deliverance one only lays hold of the name of Buddha in order to plant the seed of goodness in the heart. But it is also far from any danger of ever falling back and far above having neither thought or no-thought [Chap. V. 22]. Therefore once we meet Buddha then we see him and hear his Law and can enter into the stages of the Mahayana and Perfect Schools.

2. 下品下生 The Lowest class in the elementary stage. According to the Sutra of 16 reflections after

12 great kalpas the Lotus flower opens [i. e. deliverance takes place]

3. 下品中生 The second class in the elementary stage when the Lotus opens after 6 kalpas.

4. 下品上生 The highest class of the elementary stage, when the Lotus opens in seven times seven days.

5. 下品中生 The lowest class of the intermediate stage, when after seven days they have the joy of hearing the Law and becoming Su-to-yuen [Srotapana].

6. 下品下生 The second class of the intermediate stage when after seven days the Lotus opens, they rejoice in hearing the Law and in becoming Su-to-yuen.

7. 中品上生 The highest class of the intermediate stage. This is when at death they see Buddha and worship him and before they have lifted up their head from worship they are already translated to Paradise, the Lotus immediately opens, they hear the four great truths [Chap. IX. 3] and become Arhats [Chap. X. 11].

8. 上品下生 The lowest class of the first stage. Here in one day and one night the Lotus flower opens and in seven days they behold Buddha dimly. After three seven days more they see him clearly. After three small kalpas everything is clear having attained the state of gladness [Chap. XII. 5].

9. 上品中生 The second class of the advanced stage. This is on the purple Gold Terrace like a great precious Lotus which opens after a night. In

seven days they get the supreme wisdom which cannot be lost again.

10. 上品上生 The highest class of the advanced stage. This is when during the snapping of fingers one is born in that Pure Land kingdom where one sees the Buddha, hears the Law and gets fully enlightened without need of any patience and gets enrolled among the Buddhas.

[NOTE. **Mr. Yang of Nanking, one of the best living authorities on Chinese Buddhism, says that Nos. 11, 12, 13 of this Chapter should not have been added.**]

11. 方便有餘淨土 The Pure Land of abundant goodness. This is where the good of the three schools meet on common ground. The great discourse on Wisdom and Salvation says, besides the three realms there is the realm of the Pure Land where all the followers of the Hinayana and the Middle schools are born with the nature and the body of the Law?

Speaking generally of those born in the Pure Land of goodness there are nine classes of them:—

[1] Those of the degree of Arhat in the Tsang Kiao [Hinayana] [Chap. X. 11].

[2] Those of the degree of Pratyeka Buddha in the Tsang Kiao [Chap. X. 12] These though they speak of themselves as having attained and everlasting highest Nirvana are not aware that they still have mortal bodies, but having fallen into the Calm of immaterial waters are as if drunk and as if mad,

waiting for the wine of peace and joy to end, and then follow the enlightenment of contemplation. This is called the means of imperfect purity.

[3] The hearers of the Broad school [Tung Kiao].

[4] Those of the Pratyeka Buddha degree in the Tung Kiao school [Chap. X. 8].

[5] Those of the seventh degree of Pusa, of advanced wisdom, i.e. Arhat of the Tung Kiao [Chap. XI. 7].

[6] Those Pusas above the seventh degree of the Pie Kiao [Mahayana] [Chap. XII. 5].

[7] Those Pusas of the degree of the Ten Characteristics.

[8] Those Pusas of the degree of the Ten Returns.

[9] Those Pusas above the seventh Faith degree in the Yuen Kiao [Perfect school.]

12 實報莊嚴淨土 The Pure Land of glorious and real recompense.

Speaking generally it cultivates the motives of virtue—the real recompense. It is said to be where the mind is free and the body difficult to describe as each pore of the skin is full of Buddhist temples, does not leave the Kchana[?] for ten generations. This also may be divided into nine degrees beginning with the grades like X. 2 and ending with the highest Mysterious Enlightenment.

13 常寂光淨土 The Pure Land of eternal Calm-Light.

Speaking generally it cultivates the manifestations of virtue—the true and real spiritual nature. It is said the Archetype and Wisdom are not different things. According to right perfection both conventional truth and custom of the world are wrong, self and others are one. All matter is vanity it is not the spiritual; all thought embraces past and present. What is eternal is the spiritual. What is quiet is deliverance. What gives light is supreme wisdom. These three attributes of eternity, deliverance and light are secret treasures neither open nor locked, all-sufficient to make one eternally glad in holiness.

CHAPTER XV

THE HIGHEST RESULT OF ALL THE SCHOOLS —BUDDHAHOOD 圓極果位門

This is the highest Mysterious Enlightenment of the Perfect School. It is the perfectly full wisdom which cannot add more; the very highest real recompense of Calm-Light where the human is lost in the spiritual and principles and the knowledge of them are One.

Buddhahood is enlightenment of self and of others. It is also enlightenment and action both perfect and full. But this self-knowledge is different from that of ordinary men and knowledge of others is different from that of the two conveyances. Full enlightenment is different from that of the Pusas for this penetrates throughout the Buddhaships of the four schools. But in the Tsang Kiao and the Tung Kiao [the Hinayana and the Union Schools] Buddha only gets three enlightenments from the Buddhist truths. In the Different School [Mahayana] although he gets three kinds of enlightenment since they are of different degrees and do not reach the very fountain of things they cannot be called full enlightenment. But only the Perfect School is able to reach the very utmost of the true nature of all laws and the attainment of the very heart of things, therefore it is called the Perfect and Full Wisdom [PU TI] and what is called the very highest is to discover that all living beings come from a principle which cannot be added to one iota, therefore it is said we return to where nothing more can be got!

By the practice of this School to the utmost degree a common man beginning in ignorance, doubt and suffering should attain to the three attainments—wisdom, deliverance and the eternal state [Chap. XII. 7]. These three attainments are like seeds and also like a good soil which by action and re-action each produce infinite results. These results are called the very highest Pure Land of real recompense. There is no virtue nor attainment outside that of the spiritual life itself. This spiritual life springs from the three reflections of the Perfect Mystery and is able to remove the three doubts and reveal the three truths of life. Outside this wisdom there are no other truths. Outside truth there is no other wisdom. This is called the very highest Pure Land of Calm Light. There is no spiritual life outside of virtue. For the Mysterious nature of the Archetype of the treasures of Ju Lai are contained in all living beings—eternally the same—without birth or death, governing everything, therefore there is nothing which has not this eternal nature in it. But the Eternal Treasure nature does not change, adapting itself to new conditions. It creates all worlds therefore there is nothing in all the worlds which is not the result of its goodness.

But when reason rules, the practice of religion is like going up stream; when Buddha rules in one's heart then it is like beginning to go with the stream. The end of cultivating religion with the stream is the highest attainment of Mysterious Enlightenment. Reason is pure hard work like going up stream. Mysterious Enlightenment is pure ease like going down stream. Between them there are four steps of mutual service.

[1] When thought suddenly loses itself it is called going up stream; when thought is enlightened it is called going with the stream. Although these two methods are different, they both arise from the soul not from outside of it. Know this, that from eternity to eternity there is not one being whether saint or common man who does not each moment use these two means of cultivating religion and who do for one moment dispense with the soul of these attributes. Therefore the attainment of the soul and its powers by all the Buddhas is the soul and power which all living beings originally possess. It is like a golden image of Buddha or a golden carved serpent. The gold is the same in both and the skill of the artist is the same. Alas! there are forms in the world which are neither golden forms of a Buddha or of a serpent, but there are none which are not made out of the soul of the universe; therefore it is necessary in every thought to understand this principle.

By this enlightenment of others there is no fear that the practice of enlightenment will not become perfect. And when perfect what else is there superior to this One Soul and the right use of its powers?

THE END.